· A HISTORY LOVER'S ·
GUIDE TO

ALEXANDRIA
AND **SOUTH**
FAIRFAX COUNTY

• A HISTORY LOVER'S •
GUIDE TO

ALEXANDRIA
AND SOUTH
FAIRFAX COUNTY

LAURA A. MACALUSO

THE
History
PRESS

Published by The History Press
Charleston, SC
www.historypress.com

All images are courtesy of the author unless otherwise indicated.

Cover images:
Edmonson Sisters Monument by Erik Blome, 2010.
Lantern on historic house in Alexandria.
Costumed re-enactor on the grounds of Carlyle House.
Bird's Eye View of Alexandria, Va., Charles Magnus Publisher. *Library of Congress.*
Christ Church, Detroit Photographic Co., 1902. *Library of Congress.*
Exterior of George Washington's Mount Vernon, showing roofline and cupola.

First published 2022

ISBN 9781540252043

Library of Congress Control Number: 2022931315

*For everyone in Alexandria who works every day—in many shapes and forms—
to sustain the practice of preserving history and keep it moving forward.*

At Alexandria…the Potomac rolls its majestic stream with sublimity and grandeur, sixty-gunships may lie before the town, which stands upon its lofty banks, commanding, to a great extent, the flatter shore of Maryland. This town is rapidly on the increase, and…cannot fail of becoming one of the first cities of the new world.

—*Marquis de Chastellux,* Travels in North America, *vol. 3,* 1780–82

CONTENTS

PREFACE

his book was prepared during the COVID pandemic of 2020–22. To undertake the book work in a socially distanced and safe way, I relied heavily on Alexandria's excellent media sources, which included both print and digital references, such as the *Zebra, Alexandria Gazette Packet, Alexandria Times, Alexandria Living Magazine, Northern Virginia Magazine, Mount Vernon Gazette, VIP Alexandria Magazine,* Visit Alexandria and its digital media arm, ALXnow. Alexandria sustains a good number of publications about local news for its active and engaged citizenry and for the many people and organizations who believe in using words and pictures to tell the city's important stories. But it is not an easy time for journalism and "print" media, as the recent crowdfunding campaign to support the city's oldest news source, the *Alexandria Gazette Packet*, demonstrates. Fortunately, their crowdfunding campaign was a success, raising almost $50,000 to keep the local news organization going.

While I was not able to make full use of library or archival collections due to COVID closures, many museums and historic sites began reopening in limited ways in the early months of 2021. Groups and organizations around the city and county also began offering walking and biking tours specializing in unique historical subjects. In a few months, with both spring and vaccinations coming, I was able to enjoy and learn about Alexandria from the Manumission Tour Company, Alexandria Pedestrian and Biking Organization, Fairfax County Park Authority, Washington Area Discovery Hikes and Old Town North Tours, among others. Educational tours focused on Black history, women's history, public art, gardens and green spaces, historic preservation, the Civil War and some of the area's unique neighborhoods, such as Old Town North, Del Ray and Parker-Gray. This layered and often intersecting history demonstrates the avenues through which Alexandria can be understood and embraced, preserved and celebrated.

In addition, even though I lived in Alexandria in Fairfax County—not in the city of Alexandria proper—city leadership allowed me to attend the Alexandria City Academy, one of the many organizations through which the city encourages civic knowledge and participation. The City of Alexandria, in fact, runs several free citizen academies, including the Fire, Police, Eco, Senior and Commonwealth Attorney Academies. If you are a resident of the city and want to learn more about the different academies and when to apply, visit www.alexandriava.gov/Academies.

There are hundreds of different ways to start a book about a place like Alexandria, Virginia. The city and its surrounding areas are so rich in local and national history that it is hard to know where to turn first. A typical overview of Alexandria often reads something like this blurb from Visit Alexandria, the city's active tourism agency:

Named a Top 5 Best Small City in the U.S. 2020 for three consecutive years by the Condé Nast Traveler Readers' Choice Awards and one of the South's Best Cities 2020 by Southern Living, *Alexandria hums with a cosmopolitan feel and a walkable lifestyle—a welcoming weekend escape next to our nation's capital. A nationally designated historic district founded in 1749, Old Town Alexandria is home to more than 200 independent restaurants and boutiques alongside intimate historic museums and new happenings at the waterfront. At the heart of it all is bustling King Street, a walkable mile recognized as one of the "Great Streets" of America. New restaurants tucked into 18th- and 19th-century architecture still intact from the city's days as George Washington's hometown ignite historic and off-the-beaten-path neighborhoods as the waterfront district evolves with new energy.*

It makes you want to visit or even move here, right? While all of this and more is true about the small city on the Potomac River—even more so in the second decade of the twenty-first century—Alexandria is in the middle of its own self-examination. This is due to pressures brought on by development; climate change; economic and social disparities in health, education and housing; and the changing nature of how history is used by the city for education and tourism. Unlike many communities across the country, Alexandria and its citizens take green spaces, historic preservation and history seriously. These are not "add-ons" to city discussions, considered a "nicety" and given a once-in-a-while nod from political leadership. As Patricia Washington, the president and CEO of Visit Alexandria recently said, "History and architectural backdrop is one of the 'pillars' of tourism….Authenticity is a huge draw for tourists." The practice of public history is central to Alexandria's identity, and although there may be a struggle about how it will look in the future (and who pays and how to pay for it), there is no question about its central role in helping make the city an attractive place to live, providing employment, recreation and educational experiences for both residents, students and tourists alike.

What makes this book timely is the fact that Alexandria is at a crossroads and is aware enough to know that the choices made today will affect generations to come. While this could be said about any growing urban center at any point in time, *A History Lover's Guide to Alexandria and South Fairfax County* captures some of these changes from the busy 2020s. There have been many books written about Alexandria, but they are now, in some respects, out of date. Historical interpretation, exhibition and presentation are evolving across the nation and the world, and they have evolved in Alexandria, too. I expect that one day, this book will also be outdated, but it will also exist to document what the city and county were doing at this moment in time— their hopes, plans and ideas for a better Alexandria and how to use history to serve the city's many different needs.

A History Lover's Guide to Alexandria and South Fairfax County is designed as a snapshot of some of the city's most well-known historic places and stories and some of the newest to join the lot. It is not comprehensive, but it is a new guide to an old city, coming not from an insider but from a history lover with fresh eyes. It is also the first book, as far as I know, to showcase the connections between Alexandria the city and Alexandria in the county and to embrace the links between history, people and places.

If you are looking for your subject of particular passion—Black history, Civil War history, George Washington, women's history or archaeology, et cetera, you won't be disappointed in Alexandria, and I hope you won't be disappointed with this book. Throughout this book, I have highlighted the newest scholarship and the newest books to further your reading if you desire. In addition, there is also a bibliography that provides some standard books for your own local history library. If, like me, you desire a taste of some of the most interesting places to visit in Alexandria, this book should serve to inspire your own travels. The best advice I can provide—once you've read chapters 1 and 2—is to select a place of interest and go there. You won't be disappointed when you turn a corner and inevitably find something unexpected, something more to see. Alexandria is like that. Around every single corner is another story from history to uncover. There is almost no end to the people and places of interest here. Follow your curiosity!

ACKNOWLEDGEMENTS

I only had the pleasure of living in Alexandria for a short time, but it was well worth the effort to be here and experience the historic city and its environs. The person who got me here, as usual, was Jeffrey Nichols. He is the historian in the house. Deep gratitude also goes to Kate Jenkins, an acquisitions editor at The History Press who showed a steadfast sense of direction, stability and generosity when this writer needed it most. Thanks also to George Washington's Mount Vernon for allowing me to do mansion house history interpretation during the very hot summer of 2021. I now know what it is like to help move 1,500 people through a house tour every day during a pandemic. It was a privilege to interpret this place and its objects, such as the key to the Bastille, for visitors who shared their enthusiasm and excitement. Thanks also to Amber Nightingale Sultane and Victoria Nightingale, fellow culture, book and thrift store lovers with whom I closed my time in Alexandria.

LAND ACKNOWLEDGEMENT

As a researcher and writer, I acknowledge, commemorate and celebrate the heritage of the Indigenous people, whose ancestral lands are along the Potomac River—the name derived from the Algonquian *Patomeck*—and rivers, creeks and tributaries of the Chesapeake Bay in what is called the City of Alexandria and South Fairfax County today.

1

SOME ALEXANDRIA FACTS AND STATS TO GET STARTED

A history of the land might begin with a piece of petrified wood that is about two million years old. The hard-as-nails artifact can be found in a case inside the Dora Kelley Nature Center in Alexandria (visit for walking nature trails along Holmes Run Creek). The center has a full-wall hand-painted nature mural. Only artistic murals and maybe a visit to a solitary swampy place, such as Huntley Meadows (see chapter 8), can give us some glimpse into what the Earth was like before humans arrived on the scene. The long relationship between humans and nature is perhaps best highlighted in the City of Alexandria's herbarium, kept in shape by Rod Simmons, a longtime plant ecologist and the natural resource manager for the City of Alexandria. The fact that the city maintains an active herbarium collection—that is, a record of plants in a given area, useful for determining changes over time—is an indicator of just how much Alexandria values its natural and cultural environment. A herbarium is a museum of natural history, often containing specimens, reference books and photographic collections. Alexandria is known for being "floristically diverse," due to its varied landscape of tidal marsh and river flood plains. Alexandria's herbarium is part of a consortium of eleven herbaria in Virginia that are now digitized in a publicly accessible database of approximately three hundred thousand specimens. You can search the collections for Alexandria, Virginia, and regions well beyond the area: www.sernecportal.org/portal/.

THIS PETRIFIED LOG WAS DISCOVERED IN OCTOBER 1967 AT THE SITE OF JOHN ADAMS MIDDLE SCHOOL IN ALEXANDRIA, VIRGINIA. THE SMITHSONIAN INSTITUTION VERIFIED THAT IT CAME FROM A CONIFEROUS TREE, CUPRESSINOXYLON, THAT GREW IN THIS AREA DURING THE CRETACEOUS PERIOD, ABOUT 100 MILLION YEARS AGO.

Above: The interpretative sign on the encased petrified wood reads: "This petrified log was discovered in October 1967 at the site of John Adams Middle School in Alexandria, Virginia. The Smithsonian Institution verified that it came from a coniferous tree, *Cupressinoxylon*, that grew in this area during the Cretaceous Period, about 100 million years ago." (Dora Kelley Nature Park, Alexandria, Virginia.)

Left: Specimen of *Anacardiaceae* (sumac family) from the Franconia Bog in Fairfax County. Identified in 1844, collected by R.H. Simmons on October 25, 2003. The bog is a point of interest for its unique natural habitat and for the fact that most bogs in Alexandria and Fairfax County disappeared in the twentieth century due to development.

Wildlife of the Dora Kelley Nature Park, Maryanne Warner, 1980.

Virginia has a robust and contemporary Indigenous population, as seen in the newest place to experience contemporary Indigenous culture, the Intertribal Creatives Collective in Old Town, but Indigenous people have thousands of years of history here. Most Americans have heard the name Pocahontas, the favorite daughter of the Powhatan chief who married John Rolfe, gave birth to a son, traveled to London, died and was buried there. Virginia's relationship to Indigenous people has been complicated and intertwined from the start, whether you consider its beginnings the English settlement of Jamestown in 1607 or the European, mostly Portuguese and Spanish, exploration of the Atlantic world during the preceding century. The Captain John Smith Chesapeake National Historic Trail is a great way to explore this early history, which encompasses the Chesapeake Bay Region in Delaware, Maryland, New York, Pennsylvania, Virginia and Washington, D.C. (see www.nps.gov/cajo/index).

Modern-day Alexandria is not far from Great Falls National Historical Park, a massive gorge on the Potomac River that prevented people in ships of any kind from moving up the river. Indigenous communities were drawn to the Potomac River due to its plentiful fish, which they caught

A silver badge made by order of the Virginia General Assembly, circa 1662, with "Ye King of" engraved on one side and the name of the tribe, "Patomeck" (Potomac), engraved on the other. *Photograph by Meg E. Eastman, courtesy of the Virginia Museum of History and Culture, 1842.1.*

with fishhooks and lures made from natural materials. Moving through the area with the seasons, these Indigenous people did not leave much behind in terms of living sites or objects. The Alexandria History Museum at the Lyceum does have a piece of a large handmade vessel, which may have been a cooking pot, on display. According to one source, by the time of the American Revolution, the closest known Indigenous village to Alexandria was Namoraughquend on the Potomac River. This village is now the location of Ronald Reagan Washington National Airport. The airport, called "National" by locals, is also home to the ruins of an early plantation called Abingdon. This area was inhabited by Indigenous people, and the site can be visited at terminal A. The Alexandria History Museum at the Lyceum has recreated objects on display, including bows and arrows, knives and fishing gear. (George Washington's step-granddaughter Ellen "Nelly" Parke Custis was born at Abingdon—her house as an adult was Woodlawn Plantation, see chapter 8.)

An evocative artifact dating from the seventeenth century exists in the Virginia Museum of History and Culture, the state's public history museum in Richmond. A silver badge inscribed with the name of the tribe, "Patomeck" (Potomac), was created by the Virginia General Assembly around 1662. This badge enabled high-status Indigenous people to travel in and out of English settlements. In terms of the English era of settlement, Alexandria was originally a tobacco-centered port city in 1749—although a trading port had been established there a dozen years earlier. The shoreline had a natural cove—since filled in—on the Potomac River. It was attractive to those with deep pockets and an interest in what is today called economic development. The John Alexander family owned this land before donating it to the town that would be called "Alexandria" after its first immigrant. Indigenous people had already developed the area for farming and settlement, and white settlers would do the same—although on a different scale altogether. Alexandria continues to be developed, and the conversation about what that development should look like centers on many political conversations in the city and county.

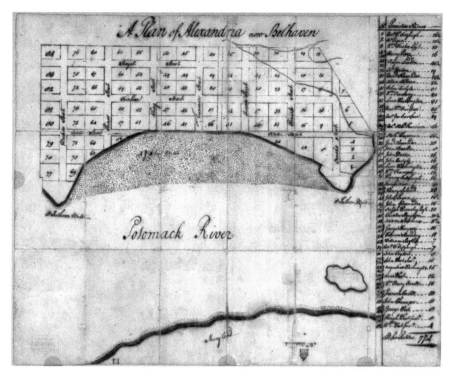

Plan of Alexandria, Now Belhaven, by George Washington, created circa 1749. *Courtesy of the Library of Congress.*

TIMELINE

13,200 years ago: Early archaeological artifacts belonging to Indigenous people in the area date to this period.

1600s: The first documented meetings between Indigenous people and Captain John Smith take place.

1749: Alexandria is established and named for John Alexander, a wealthy Scottish immigrant (and the reason why the city celebrates its Scottish heritage with the Scottish Christmas Walk and plenty of tartan). The "port city" starts a lucrative tobacco trade.

1783: The Alexandria Masonic Lodge is chartered, with George Washington as its founding member.

1789: A portion of Northern Virginia, including Alexandria and Arlington, is ceded to the new capital city, Washington, District of Columbia, creating a diamond-shaped city on both banks of the Potomac River.

1830s: At least five thousand enslaved people are brought into Alexandria via Franklin & Armfield, the most successful slave-trading business of the antebellum era.

1846: Virginia asks for the return of Virginian lands, due to a deepening rift between the states heading toward abolitionism and the states keeping a slave economy intact.

1850s: The first Jewish immigrants arrive in Alexandria.

1861–65: The U.S. Army occupies Alexandria for the duration of the Civil War, using the city as a transportation depot, supply center, military hospital center and defense center for the U.S. capital. Colonel Elmer E. Ellsworth pulls down Confederate flag from the Marshall Building and is shot and killed. The town becomes a refuge for fugitive enslaved people. The Lee-Fendall House and the Carlyle House are two of the many structures that were turned into hospitals. By the end of the war, Alexandria was devastated; it would take decades to rebuild its economy and infrastructure.

1892: The first electric streetcar system in the country is opened for tourists to travel to Mount Vernon.

1918: The end of World War I—15,600 died in Virginia from the "great influenza" pandemic.

1925: The first traffic light becomes operational at King and Washington Streets.

1939: The Alexandria Library Sit-In, the first "sit-in" in American civil rights history, occurs.

1946: Alexandria becomes the third city in the United States to establish a National Historic District to preserve its architectural heritage.

1960s: Alexandria schools are integrated. The first municipal archaeological commission in the United States is formed. Landmark Center (later Mall) opens. The Historic Alexandria Foundation begins its early building survey plaque program, which places bronze markers on historic houses that are at least one hundred years old. This was done in response to architectural teardowns of the urban renewal era.

1967: Alexandria lawyer Bernie Cohen leads the prosecution of *Loving v. Virginia*, which struck down the federal ban on interracial marriage.

1990s: *Remember the Titans*, a Disney feature film, depicts the story of the Titans football team from T.C. Williams High School, the first integrated high school in the city.

2019–2020: Alexandria suffers from a "hundred-year flood" three times in one year, highlighting climate change and an outdated storm

Death of Col. Ellsworth After Hauling Down the Rebel Flag, at the Taking of Alexandria, Va., May 24th, 1861, Currier & Ives, circa 1861. *Courtesy of the Library of Congress.*

system. The city purchases Freedom House Museum and prepares new exhibits. Amazon announces that its new HQ2 will be built in Arlington, along its border with Alexandria. Virginia Tech chooses to build "Innovation Campus" in Alexandria. *Appomattox*, a Confederate monument, is removed from its pedestal at the intersection of Prince and Washington Streets.

2021: Alexandria experiences more flooding throughout the year. The Virginia Historical Highway Marker in front of Robert E. Lee's boyhood home is removed for rewriting. T.C. Williams High School is renamed Alexandria City High School (Williams was a segregationist). Other school and street names with a Confederate association are under consideration for renaming.

POPULATION

There are approximately 160,000 residents in the city of Alexandria, and more than one million people live in Fairfax County, a number that continues to grow. According to one source, Alexandria is the densest jurisdiction in the Commonwealth of Virginia, with recent growth in the twenty-first century putting more pressure on its transportation infrastructure, economic development and city services. The area is home to 13 percent of all Virginians, and Virginia is geographically a large state. In the city of Alexandria, the population has grown by about 1 percent since 2010; this is predicted to translate to 214,000 people by 2050. Demonstrating the growth of the city of Alexandria and bleeding into South Fairfax County, there are nine zip codes attached to Alexandria: 22301, 22302, 22304, 22305, 22306, 22311, 22312, 22314 and 22315.

NEIGHBORHOODS OF ALEXANDRIA AND AREAS OF SOUTH FAIRFAX COUNTY

The neighborhoods of the city of Alexandria include Old Town, Old Town North, Waterfront, Del Ray, Carlyle/Eisenhower East, National Landing and Potomac Yard, North Ridge, West End, Seminary Hill, Landmark, Parkfairfax, Arlandria, Rosemont and Parker-Grey. "Below the Beltway" in South Fairfax County are the neighborhoods of Franconia, Rose Hill, Kingstowne, Huntington, Belle Haven, Fort Hunt, Hybla Valley and Groveton and Mount Vernon. Farther south in the county are the areas of Mason Neck and Lorton. This book will touch on some of these distinct areas.

HOLIDAYS AND CELEBRATIONS IN ALEXANDRIA

Alexandria is awash in celebrations and commemorations that last all year long. This is a town that likes to celebrate, march and gather as a community. Starting early in the year, Alexandria gears up for Presidents Day, which is called George Washington Day in Alexandria. There's actually a whole month dedicated to the first president, and the event is chaired by the George Washington Birthday Celebration Commission. Coinciding with Black History Month, there are plenty of special tours and programs dedicated to both subjects available around the city. Early spring is cherry blossom season, and Alexandria gets in on Washington, D.C.'s game by hosting cherry blossom–themed restaurant events and boat tours to the Tidal Basin and back, reconnecting the two cities every year. The first cherry blossoms were planted at the Tidal Basin in Washington, D.C., in 1912, when three thousand plants were gifted to the capital city by Tokyo, Japan.

Spring also brings the annual Historic Gardens Week, hosted by the Garden Club of Virginia. As a town known for its charm and historic environment, the city of Alexandria is always included as a day event during Historic Garden Week. Visitors can purchase tickets to enter the private gardens and homes of residents who decorate according to a theme or style. The summer season brings wine festivals at George Washington's Mount Vernon, as well as Fourth of July celebrations there and at many of the smaller historic house museums in the city. July 10 is also the City of Alexandria's birthday, and fireworks and celebrations coincide with Fourth of July celebrations. In late fall comes the Around the World Cultural Food Festival. Finally, Alexandria is a serious destination for the Christmas season: the Scottish Christmas Walk, where family clans, such as the Frasers, turn out to march with fifes and drums in tartan kilts, comes in early December.

HOW TO GET AROUND ALEXANDRIA

Alexandria is fortunate to have access to various modes of transportation beyond the automobile.

PLANES AND TRAINS

Old Town Alexandria is less than five miles away from Ronald Reagan National Airport. Dulles International Airport is thirty-five miles away in Loudon County. In addition to flights, Alexandria is also a regular stop on Amtrak. If you are traveling south or coming up from the southern states to Alexandria, you can take your car on Amtrak's Auto Train, which runs from Lorton in South Fairfax County to Florida. The Virginia Railway Express serves commuters and stops at King Street Station, serves Amtrak and goes on to Union Station in Washington, D.C. Finally, the Metro takes commuters and visitors between Alexandria and Washington, D.C. There are four stops in Alexandria, including King Street–Old Town (yellow and blue lines), Braddock Road (yellow and blue lines), Eisenhower Avenue (yellow line) and Van Dorn (blue line).

BIKING AND BUSES

There is no shortage of biking trails in Alexandria and South Fairfax County. Both the city and county have put a lot of emphasis on creating trails, paved pathways and designating streets for bikers. One of the two trails of note are the Mount Vernon Trail, which travels from Rosslyn (across the Potomac River from Washington, D.C.) to Mount Vernon, crossing through Alexandria, and is used by commuters and recreational bikers alike. The other is the Fairfax Cross County Connector, which takes bikers to South Fairfax County sites, including Mount Vernon, Telegraph Road, Huntley Meadows, Richmond Highway and Franconia Highway. Alexandria supports the Capital Bikeshare Program, in which you can rent a bike and go wherever you want all over Northern Virginia and even into Washington, D.C., and Maryland. The bright-red bikes are hard to miss. The biking community of Alexandria is active—there are several bike shops in Old Town and the county (this author's favorite is Rat's Cycles in Springfield), and hosted rides include the Tour d'Alexandria (a tour of the libraries in Alexandria) and the Tour de Mount Vernon, which happens in the fall every year, visiting historic sites and Fort Belvoir. In addition, the Alexandria Bicycle and Pedestrian Advisory Committee arranges bike safety workshops and special holiday-themed bike tours year-round, including a Halloween Decorations in Del Ray Ride, a Presidential History Ride and a Women's History Ride.

If biking is not your thing, DASH (Driving Alexandria Safely Home) is Alexandria's bus system. In Fairfax County, the Fairfax Connector is part of the mass transportation system, connecting passengers to the Metro and other bus lines.

WATER TAXIS AND TROLLEYS

At Alexandria's Waterfront, you can pick up a water taxi to the National Harbor, Georgetown, the Wharf and Audi Field; traveling south on the Potomac River, the taxis reach Mount Vernon. The Potomac Water Taxi connects with a ten-minute walk to the Tidal Basin and is popular during cherry blossom season. Old Town features a free King Street Trolley, stopping at locales around town.

While all of these transportation options are useful, as one tour guide said to this author, "If you want to see Alexandria, you need to walk Alexandria." So, whatever method you've got access to—legs, wheelchair, bicycle, stroller—the important thing is to get out of your car and experience the city from street level. This is not always easy for people with mobility impairments, wheelchairs or strollers, due to the historic nature of the streets, but long sections of waterfront parks and the Mount Vernon Trail provide smooth surfaces for all. Also, be sure to be aware of what is below your feet: cobblestones, mounting blocks—for stepping in/out of carriages or onto horses—and boot scrapers, all authentic historic details, are common in Old Town. So, street level is where the action happens.

2

A SHORT SERIES OF ALEXANDRIA HISTORY STORIES

Amid all the building and rebuilding for the future, Alexandria is finding ways to embrace a varied and eventful past—history that is both full of inspiration and, sometimes, desperation. Peel back the charms of Old Alexandria to learn about the nuances of life at the crossroads of the Atlantic, between the North and South and between the old and the new. The following are three recent historical stories that are equal parts Alexandria: "The Old Town Armada"; "Harriet Jacobs and Free Education for All"; and "Name Changes and Monument Removals."

STORY 1: THE OLD TOWN ARMADA

The maritime history and heritage of Alexandria keeps coming into focus with new archaeological discoveries. Perhaps it shouldn't come as a surprise that a place called the "Port City" produces so much material, but to twenty-first-century eyes, few discoveries bring the past to life in the same way that finding a buried ship does. Where else in the Mid-Atlantic have so many historic ships been discovered buried under city streets? Alexandria has even contemplated making an entirely new Waterfront Museum dedicated to the three hundred–plus years of maritime history there, just to do the story justice. Beginning life as a port city, Alexandria was a major seaport long before the Revolutionary War. But it is the city's continued economic

View From Pioneer Mill, Looking Up the Wharf, photograph by Andrew J. Russell, May 1865. *Courtesy of the Library of Congress.*

development that is the key reason so much material is discovered in the ground. The new development often means new digging and thus new discoveries. The fact that Alexandria has professional archaeologists on staff means that this material is identified, cared for and studied.

One early method of economic development in waterfront towns was intentionally sinking ships, which would act as foundation material to pile earth, stone and fill on, literally creating new ground. In other words, many shorelines up and down the Atlantic have been manipulated to grow (or recede, if needed) by developers. This is true of places like the Back Bay in Boston and New Haven, Connecticut (when you drive I-95, hugging the shoreline, you are traveling over such fill). In early 2021, a new riverfront development in Alexandria called Robinson Landing unearthed 150,000 new artifacts, plus three nineteenth-century wooden ships. The so-called Old Town Armada was not the first such discovery, but it was the largest, and in addition to the hulls themselves, evocative maritime artifacts, such as an almost complete ship's biscuit, have been found. The ships were found to be the *Emily Washington* from 1810, the *Plumie E. Smith* from 1811 and an unnamed ship. An earlier unnamed vessel from 1836 was the first to be discovered in another area of the waterfront. More discoveries included privies, wells, foundations, wharves and more.

Alexandria was already fortunate regarding the study of maritime history. The logbook to a schooner called the *Enterprize* has helped historians understand the seagoing merchant class of Alexandria, whose wealth helped create the city. Dating from 1803–4, the logbook documents three trading voyages to the Caribbean and one to Spain and France. The schooner, sixty-three feet long and twenty feet wide, was built in Glastonbury, Connecticut, but belonged to a collective of three merchants from Alexandria. Because of the period and location, the *Enterprize* engaged in the Triangular Trade—it didn't carry humans in slavery, but it traded the goods that were part of the economic relationship between the United States, Europe and the Caribbean. For example, the sugar and rum, sweeteners desired by everyone, brought back to Alexandria were made in harrowing circumstances by enslaved Africans and their descendants in the Caribbean. The logbook of the *Enterprize* is a rare survivor, detailing life and work onboard an early nineteenth-century ship.

STORY 2: HARRIET JACOBS AND FREE EDUCATION FOR ALL

The history of education in Alexandria is rich and varied across time, dating to at least George Washington and his support for an "Alexandria Academy," which was chartered by the Virginia Assembly in 1786. It was intended as a school that would serve poor whites, orphans and women, students not usually included in early American education. Washington himself did not receive a full formal education due to the death of his father when he was eleven. He took self-learning seriously, developing a large library at Mount Vernon, and he became a benefactor of this school. Later, Robert E. Lee received his first years of formal education at the Alexandria Academy. From 1812 to 1847, there existed a "Free Colored School" within the building, sponsored by free Black people. As Tamika Nunley describes in her book *At the Threshold of Liberty, Women, Slavery and Shifting Identities in Washington, D.C.* (Chapel Hill: University of North Carolina Press, 2021), formerly enslaved individuals often provided the backing for schools, and for girls especially, going to school pushed the accepted boundaries. The free school was closed when Alexandria was ceded back to the Commonwealth of Virginia, which did not allow formal

"Colored school at Alexandria, 1864, taught by Harriet Jacobs and daughter agents of New York Friends Emory University." *Courtesy of the Robert Langmuir African American Photograph Collection, circa 1840–2000, Education-Elementary and Secondary Rose Library Emory University.*

education for Black Americans. In 1884, the school building was absorbed into the city's public school system. You can see a marker for the original location of the school at the intersection of Washington and Wolfe Streets.

While this was a strong start for public education in Alexandria, the story of Harriet Jacobs fulfills the desire of free education for all. Jacobs (1813 or 1815–1897) was born into slavery in North Carolina. Showing resistance to her enslaver, who sexually harassed her, Jacobs hid for seven years in an attic until she could escape north to New York. During the Civil War and after, Jacobs traveled back to the South, establishing schools for fugitive and newly freed Black Americans in Alexandria. By the time Jacobs had opened and was running the Jacobs School, she had already written her autobiography, titled *Incidents in the Life of a Slave Girl*. Although she wrote under the name Linda Brent, Jacobs became known in abolitionist circles. Published in 1861 at the beginning of the war, the book is now considered a classic example of literature written by an enslaved person and is used by museum and historic site staff for its direct account of daily life for enslaved people. Amazingly, a photograph of one of her schools survives in the special archives collection of Emory University.

From a letter dated one year after the school was established in Alexandria—and close to the end of the Civil War—Jacobs wrote:

Alexandria, Jan. 13, 1865
I must say one word about our school. While we were very fitting up in the house, the scholars were very much scattered in other schools, particularly the most advanced scholars. Within the new year, many of them have come back.

My daughter's health will not allow her to be confined to the school. She has charge of the Industrial Department, is teacher in the Sabbath School, and assists me in my out-door work. We need another teacher.

The school is making progress under the charge of their teachers. It is the largest, and I am anxious it, shall be the best. The New-York and Pennsylvania associations are establishing new schools in Alexandria. All seem to be well attended.

STORY 3: MONUMENT REMOVALS AND NAME CHANGES

The problem of Confederate monument culture was visited and revived in the years of social unrest following the race-driven murders in Charleston, South Carolina, in 2015 and the Unite the Right Rally on the University of Virginia's campus in 2017. Confederate monument removals and name changes to schools began to speed up across the South. Alexandria, a crossroads community if there ever was one, was not immune to these historic changes. But with the death of George Floyd in May 2020 in Minneapolis, protests spread across the country, and many felt the pressure to remove Confederate symbols in the public square. Since 1889, Alexandria has had such a symbol standing in a public place: *Appomattox*, a bronze standing figure of a Confederate soldier, with its head gazing downward, was named for that place in central Virginia where Robert E. Lee surrendered to Ulysses S. Grant on April 9, 1865.

Only a month after Floyd's death, the United Daughters of the Confederacy (UDC), which owned the monument, removed the bronze figure and placed it in storage. Located at a busy intersection of Prince and Washington Streets in Old Town, this is the spot from which men with Confederate sympathies left Alexandria before it was taken over by the United States Army at the start of the war. The lone figure was unusual for a Confederate monument—a man with his arms folded, looking down toward the ground. Was he referencing the loss of so many men during four years of bloody warfare, or was he lamenting the loss of the South to the North? Despite calls for its removal for many years, *Appomattox* had remained in place due to a state law that prevented the removal of monuments dedicated to

Appomattox Monument, by Caspar Buberl (1889), commissioned by the United Daughters of the Confederacy. *Courtesy of Kristopher Grubbs, CC BY-SA 4.0, via Wikimedia Commons, www.creativecommons.org.*

veterans. The General Assembly of the Commonwealth of Virginia, under Governor Ralph Northam's administration, changed this law in early 2020, which indicated a death knell for many Confederate monuments, including *Appomattox*, which was removed on June 2, 2020. Today, after the bronze monument and its granite base were removed, the circle is now part of the blacktop pavement, and people without prior knowledge of the monument would never know it was there.

Although some monuments have been relocated to private properties, others, such as *Appomattox*, are now in storage and unlikely to see daylight for a long time to come. In 2021, Christ Church in Alexandria removed two plaque-style memorials to George Washington and Robert E. Lee from the church proper, relocating them to an annex building, where interpretation (another word for museum-style education) can be presented. The most recent monument removal was that of the Virginia Historical Highway

George Washington and Robert E. Lee memorial tablets that were removed from Christ Church and placed in the church's annex (2021).

Marker in front of the Lee Boyhood Home in Old Town. The sign was removed by the Virginia Department of Historic Resources on November 5, 2021, although the reasons given were that corrections needed to be made to mistakes present in the content. The metal sign will return with an updated text.

In addition to monument removal, the renaming of schools, parks, streets and other public spaces is something that Alexandria has been heavily engaged in throughout 2020–21. As noted in the previous timeline, T.C. Williams High School was renamed, as determined by a school board vote on July 10, 2020. A petition circulated through the city, resulting in one hundred names being presented to the board. In the end, the name Alexandria City High School was thought to be a good solution to the competing suggestions. The school was originally named for Thomas Chambliss Williams, who was the superintendent from the 1930s to the 1960s and who was noted as a segregationist. Included in that vote was a name change for other schools, including Matthew Maury Elementary School. Maury was a naval captain for the Confederacy and is recognized around the commonwealth with monuments. Other name changes are being discussed in both the city of Alexandria and Fairfax County, the most contentious being a name change for Lee Street in Alexandria and Lee Highway in Fairfax County.

Both the city and the county produced reports about the issue of names and naming. The Office of Historic Alexandria reported identifying more than 30 street names with a Confederate association. The Fairfax County History Commission produced a report in December 2020 titled "The Fairfax County Names Inventory Report." The 539-page report found approximately 157 street names, monuments and public spaces named for Confederates. For both the city and the county, this was the starting place in understanding how deeply embedded the Confederacy, via "lost cause" ideology, was in reshaping public memory. As noted by the *Alexandria Times*, Lee Street in the city was originally Water Street but was renamed after the death of Robert E. Lee's wife in 1870. In other words, place names are not written in stone, and they evolve over time to represent the interests of contemporary people. The commission recommended surveying the available literature around the social history of the Civil War, especially as experienced by Black communities, as a next step in the process of potential renaming. Both the city and county require a community engagement process before names are changed.

Not all monument removals and name changes are related to the Confederacy. In 2021, the Eisenhower Monument, which stood in the traffic circle at Eisenhower Avenue and Holland Lane, was removed due to a road reconstruction project. The monument depicted President Dwight D. Eisenhower in his army uniform—an appropriate choice for the Alexandria area, due to the location of Fort Belvoir and its long history of military installations. But the monument was really about "Ike's" role after the war, when he worked to create the interstate highway system. A new location for the Eisenhower Monument is yet to be determined.

3

A SELECTION OF OLD TOWN HISTORIC SITES

Alexandria Visitor Center in the Historic Ramsay House
221 King Street
Alexandria, VA 22314
www.visitalexandriaVA.com

Near the visitor center is the first Virginia Department of Historic Resources "Historical Highway Marker" to be highlighted in this book. These metal roadside markers, painted black and white, were an early attempt to provide history to the public for free. Sometimes called "History On a Stick," Virginia's marker program is the oldest in the country, started in 1927 on nearby Route 1, marking special spots between Richmond and Mount Vernon. The program continues, and today, more than 2,500 markers have been placed across the commonwealth to highlight historic sites, biographies and landscapes of significance.

The "Historic Alexandria" marker, placed outside the visitor center, reads:

Alexandria was named for the family of John Alexander, a Virginia planter who, in 1669, acquired the tract on which the town began. By 1732, the site was known as Hunting Creek Warehouse and, in 1749, became Alexandria, thereafter a major 18th-century port. George Washington frequented the town: Robert E. Lee claimed it as his boyhood home. From 1801 to 1847, Alexandria was part of the District of

Bronze plaque for the
Ramsay House at street
level, Alexandria.

Columbia and was later occupied by federal troops during the Civil War. By the 20ᵗʰ century, it had become a major railroad center. In 1946, Alexandria created the third historic district in the United States to protect its 18ᵗʰ- and 19ᵗʰ-century buildings.

Be sure to start your visit here. The eighteenth-century building, originally owned by William Ramsay, occupies a corner lot and features a garden in the back, where you can take a break and enjoy the sun and your surroundings. The sounds of street musicians are a given on the weekends, and restaurants, stores, historic sites, public art and the waterfront parks can all be accessed easily from the visitor center, which is, itself, a historic site. Inside, free tourist information and staff are available seven days a week.

A bronze plaque at street level indicates the authentically historic nature of the building. Ramsay knew and was involved in the mercantile business, as were John Carlyle and John Dixon, other "founding fathers" of the city. In the same year as the founding of the Town of Alexandria, Ramsay had this house shipped upriver from Dumfries, Virginia, and placed on this lot. From his vantage point on a hill overlooking the Potomac River, Ramsay could see ships coming into and out of port. Like Carlyle, Ramsay came from Scotland, and like Carlyle, he married into a prosperous family; Ann McCarthy, a cousin of George Washington, became his bride. When Ramsay died in 1785, Washington attended his funeral. In turn, when Washington died, William Ramsay's son Dennis, the mayor of Alexandria, served as a pallbearer.

The Ramsay House, like so many historic properties, had an eventful life, including time spent as a tavern, a grocery store, a boardinghouse and a cigar factory. The historic nature and corner location of the building was noted by the 1950s, when the City of Alexandria purchased it. The Ramsay House has been the official visitor center since 1956. For those with a taste for ghost hunting, Alexandria's "Original Ghost & Graveyard Tour" starts at the visitor center. If ever a city was built for walks at night with costumed guides holding lanterns, Alexandria is it. (Visit www. alexcolonialtours.com.)

Alexandria City Hall and Market Square
300–1 King Street
Alexandria, VA 22314

The stretch between Alexandria Visitor Center and Market Square is the briefest of walks. They are basically across the street from each other. But here, you are in the heart of the city, and its streets and historic buildings stretch out in every direction, luring visitors with a dozen sights. Market Square itself is, incongruously, not much to look at. In the center of the square is a modern water fountain that somewhat obscures Alexandria City Hall behind it. Originally built in 1749, the year of the town's founding, after a fire, the current city hall was reconstructed in 1871, with newer additions completed in the late twentieth century. There is also a clock tower from 1783, with a cast-iron bell that has, unfortunately, not operated for decades. According to ALXnow, the inscription on the bell reads, "Steeple, clock and bell presented to the City of his nativity by an esteemed citizen. Alexandria, VA, A.D., 1872." Bell foundries, once plentiful on both side of the Atlantic, have all but gone out of business, including the maker of the Alexandria Clock Tower bell, the Meneely Bell Foundry in New York State.

Left: *Brio*, by Jimilu Mason, in Market Square, Alexandria.

Below: Cannon-as-Fountain Memorial, a commemorative installation by the Daughters of the American Revolution.

Market Square has been here since Alexandria became a town, though, so it is worth it to take a moment and view the square. If you are fortunate enough to be in Old Town on a Saturday morning, Market Square comes alive when its farmers' market gets going. This farmers' market, the oldest continuously running market on the same site in the United States, attracts farmers from the county with fresh dairy, vegetables, flowers, baked goods and more. In one corner of Market Square stands one of the city's oldest works of public art. *Brio* was created by artist Jimilu "Mimi" Mason, a twentieth-century sculptor and a resident of the DMV (Washington metropolitan) area. *Brio* is a word that means "finesse, vigor and vivacity," and the energy of the sculpture of a male dancer suggests the same. The artist's work is in collections as varied as the Kennedy Center's and the U.S. Supreme Court's. *Brio* was donated to the City of Alexandria by the Northern Virginia Fine Arts Association.

The buildings surrounding Market Square are more new than old, but the area retains its status as a center for civic gatherings year-round. One can walk across North Royal Street from Market Square to see a French and Indian War cannon that has been repurposed as a drinking fountain. The major French and Indian War connection in Alexandria comes through General Edward Braddock and his time at Carlyle House, and this cannon may date from the ill-fated military expedition. Another cannon of this ilk is on display at the intersection of Braddock and Russell Roads. The Daughters of the American Revolution (DAR) is known for its deep patriotism and love for monument-making, and in Alexandria, the DAR took a historic cannon and turned it into a drinking fountain for the city. A bronze plaque located close by notes that the cannon drinking fountain was originally located at the corner of Fairfax and Cameron Streets, but the Mount Vernon chapter of the DAR helped move it to its present location when developers came to the Market Square area. The fountain is not all cannon, though; soldered onto the structure are two dolphins that once spurted water into the second level, a small, upper-level trough that was meant for birds and a lower trough, at ground level, that was meant for dogs. The story goes horses drank from the mid-level trough. Today, the fountain runs dry and forgotten next to the much larger modern fountain with spurting water in the center of Market Square.

Carlyle House Historic Park
121 North Fairfax Street
Alexandria, VA 22314
www.novaparks.com

The Carlyle House is a standout in many ways in Northern Virginia. First, it is owned and managed by the Northern Virginia Regional Parks Authority (NOVA Parks) and is therefore part of a major park system. This tells us there are many historical players in Alexandria, from private, not-for-profit entities, such as the Mount Vernon Ladies Association, to local government agencies, such as the Office of Historic Alexandria, which runs eleven museums in the city, including Gadsby's Tavern and the new Freedom House Museum. NOVA Parks is an important entity in the preservation of the county's history, as evinced by its efforts to save River Farm (more on that later). NOVA Parks can point to its work in preservation and interpretation of Carlyle House Historic Park to demonstrate its commitment to managing history on behalf of the public. At the Carlyle House, NOVA Parks has a lot of work to do, as this house is one of the oldest and grandest in Alexandria and Northern Virginia. It is also a house that was used (and perhaps abused) over the course of its long life, so preservation work continues.

Scottish merchant and city founder John Carlyle built the Georgian-style mansion in 1752–53. At the time, the house faced the Potomac River, which

Original keystone for Carlyle House (1752).

came much closer to the house then than it does today. Easy access to the river meant that the plantation could easily participate in trade, and Carlyle had the means to do it, as he had married into the Fairfax family. A century before, people like Mary Brent ran their homes and plantations with indentured servants. By the time of John Carlyle and Sarah Fairfax Carlyle, enslaved Africans labored in the house and on the plantation. Like many men of his generation, including George Washington and Thomas Jefferson, Carlyle inherited enslaved Black people as part of his wife's dowry.

The house is impressive in its size and scale, and it must be imagined sitting

The front door of Carlyle House decorated with a tartan wreath. Note the keystone over the door.

grandly alone, one façade facing the river and the other facing Market Square. It's no wonder General Edward Braddock decided to use Carlyle House as his campaign headquarters in 1755, during the French and Indian War. Braddock and his military advisors and strategists planned the overthrow of Fort Duquesne (now downtown Pittsburgh). George Washington volunteered to serve as an aide-de-camp to Braddock, and many future American notables were involved in the military plan, including Charles Lee and Horatio Gates. Thousands of troops came to Alexandria via the city's wharves, and Carlyle House became a raucous command center for the British (today Carlyle House staff fly the Union Jack from the façade to let potential visitors know that Braddock is in town). Unfortunately, the military plans ended in defeat, and Braddock himself died from battle wounds and was buried close to the road on retreat. Later his remains were found and reburied on what is today Fort Necessity Battlefield. Outside Carlyle House a sign titled "Historic Braddock Road," introducing visitors to this story.

Carlyle House went on to more fame a century later, when the house served as one of Alexandria's many Civil War hospitals. A hotel had been built directly in front of the already historic house, and a series of attached buildings, called the Mansion House Hospital, served the Union army, as Alexandria was an occupied city (that is, a southern city occupied by the federal government's Army of the Potomac). The made-for-the-public PBS television series *Mercy Street* is a fictionalized account of the kinds of divided loyalties, subterfuge and difficult situations that arose when those who were sympathetic to the North and those who were sympathetic to the South encountered each other—sometimes even within the same family. If Civil War–era hospitals are your thing, a free walking map can be found here: www.alexandriava.gov/uploadedFiles/historic/info/civilwar/hospitals/CivilWarHospitalsWalkingTourBrochure.pdf

A final note on John Carlyle: if you spend some time in Alexandria, you will notice its penchant for all things tartan and Scottish. This is in homage to John Carlyle and the Carlyle House and other immigrants, like William Ramsay, who quite literally put Alexandria on the map.

Alexandria History Museum at the Lyceum

201 South Washington Street
Alexandria, VA 22314
www.alexandria.gov/Lyceum

Buildings like the Lyceum were common in nineteenth-century America. Designed to be a cultural community center that would uplift citizens through lectures and libraries, the Lyceum became home to the City of Alexandria's public history collection long after it went defunct with the changing tastes of modern life in the early twentieth century. In an era before public libraries, public schools and public parks, a city with a lyceum provided its elite city residents with access to contemporary developments in the arts, science,

Left: A bust of Cicero that was purchased by the Fairfax family in Italy in the seventeenth century and installed in the Lyceum in the 1830s.

Right: A Fresnel lens light from Jones Point Park, Alexandria, in the collection of the Alexandria History Museum at the Lyceum.

music, culture and more. This idea was very much part of the culture of the first half of the nineteenth century, an era when the idea of "improvement" was on everyone's minds. Cities could be improved with new architecture, designed in a way to reflect the democratic origins of the country, and people could be improved with access to writers, scientists, artists and others who came to speak in places like lyceums. Thus, the style of architecture selected for this era of improvement was Greek Revival, which connected the United States to the classical world. In case you don't believe this, walk up the stairs of the Lyceum to the second floor and look for the marble busts of Greek philosophers placed high on the wall. The toga-wearing ancients—Marcus Tullius Cicero and Lucius Annaeus Seneca—are sitting in on one of the many talks heard in this room, one hundred–plus years ago.

The first floor of the Lyceum is a historical overview of the City of Alexandria told through objects, maps and artwork. Although the exhibits are dated, this part of the museum is engrossing, due to the variety of the objects included. Do you want to see a real tea chest, one of the products of the global trade that impacted Virginia? How about fired ceramic pots made by Black Americans? The Fresnel lens lights from the Jones Point Park Lighthouse are here and so are re-created Indigenous tools, demonstrating indigenous ways of making use of the Potomac River and its many creeks and tributaries.

An American city of the nineteenth century would have to either have a patron with very deep pockets or a blossoming economy to build something like the Lyceum on behalf of the public. Alexandria's Lyceum, with its pediment sitting on top of massive Doric columns, speaks to the success of the port city and the desire to showcase this success through a cultural statement. You can make your own cultural statement today by buying a good book or something else worthy of your funds in the museum store.

Athenaeum
201 Prince Street
Alexandria, VA 22314
www.nvfaa.org

One might think that this building, which looks like an athenaeum and functions like an athenaeum, received its name when it was erected in 1852—but this is not so. The building is a demonstration in brick, plaster and paint of Alexandria's great success as a port city during the era of maritime trade, but it was built in 1852 for the Bank of Old Dominion at the head of Captain's Row, making this a great intersection to visit and view. In between its time as a bank, the chief commissary office of the Union army, a factory space for the Stabler-Leadbeater Apothecary, a bank again and, finally, a Methodist church, the Athenaeum has led an interesting life in Alexandria, finishing in 1964 as the gallery and event space for the Northern Virginia Fine Arts Association (NVFAA), which is how it remains today.

According to the NVFAA, the building was given the name Athenaeum as a nod to the Greek goddess of wisdom, Athena. In the nineteenth century, athenaeums became popular in American society as places where people could visit art and science exhibitions and browse collections of books. In this way, they are cultural centers in the same way the Lyceum

An Atheneum interior with a contemporary art exhibit.

is, and notably, in Alexandria, as in much of the country, using the Greek Revival style to design this building made perfect sense, as it connected the young country to the ancient classical world. The building was steeped in classical associations, even if its use was commercial. A bank might also decide to build in the Greek Revival style, as its wide, solid, Doric columns on façades suggest the permanence of a business and the taste of bank owners and clients. By naming the building the Athenaeum, the NVFAA was calling on that earlier era of American culture, when famous athenaeums, such as the Wadsworth Athenaeum in Hartford, Connecticut, the Providence Athenaeum or the Boston Athenaeum, provided cities with their first art museums.

Like many buildings and open green spaces in Alexandria, the Athenaeum is rented out for weddings and special events, but otherwise, the building is open to the public and is certainly worth stepping inside— not only for its changing artwork on display but also for its two-story-tall glass windows, the wall space between the wood frames almost disappearing due to the enormous glass panes.

Murray-Dick-Fawcett House
517 Prince Street
Alexandria, VA 22314

One of newest historic houses to join the Office of Historic Alexandria's collection, the Murray-Dick-Fawcett House is also one of the oldest in the city—and it looks like the oldest home in the city. That works two ways in a historic city like Alexandria: first, the authentic condition of the house— it is considered the least-altered historic house in Northern Virginia—is recognized and valued; at the same time, in 2021, the Office of Historic Alexandria began its work to stabilize the circa-eighteenth-century house, which has only been open to the public for special occasions. A special agreement with the last owner allows the resident to continue living on site until circumstances change. In the meantime, important preservation work can begin, preventing further deterioration or structure loss.

The City of Alexandria plans to preserve the house as a center for learning about everyday life in the eighteenth and early nineteenth centuries in Alexandria. The house was built in three stages in 1772, 1784 and 1797, and it retains much of its historic fabric, including handwrought nails, original pine floors and batten doors. The first owner was a blacksmith named

The exterior of the Murray-Dick-Fawcett House.

Patrick Murray. The next was Elisha Cullen Dick, yet another Alexandria-area physician who attended George Washington on his deathbed at Mount Vernon. Finally, the John Douglass Brown family came into possession of the house in 1816 and remained its owners for 184 years, the longest tenure of any family in a house in Alexandria. A descendant of the Brown family named Lewis Fawcett began preserving the historic house when, in the 1930s, the U.S. government came to call. The Historic American Buildings Survey (HABS) crew documented the house using black-and-white photographs and plans, which can be seen digitally on the Library of Congress's website.

Stabler-Leadbeater Apothecary Museum
105–7 South Fairfax Street
Alexandria, VA 22314
www.apothecarymuseum.org

There aren't many authentic historic pharmacies or apothecaries still in existence. Florentines and visitors to Italy, for example, can go to Santa Maria Novella, the oldest known working pharmacy in the Western world, founded in 1612. Americans and visitors to the United States have the Stabler-Leadbeater Apothecary, which was operated in the same place by the same family for 141 years. Not a large space, the Stabler-Leadbeater Apothecary nevertheless packs a punch with its long, narrow cabinets decorated with Gothic tracery details and hundreds of glass jars with "[gilded] label under glass" picking up the light from the front windows.

Sitting on a counter is a stone mortar and pestle, the most essential tools for an apothecary. With a second floor filled with herbs that are sealed in small envelopes and placed in wooden drawers, an apothecary could make medicines for customers in need on the spot. When people had a health issue, they often went directly to the apothecary, not a doctor. Medicine was not highly regulated, and Americans could ask for any concoction that an apothecary was willing to sell, including one of the most common drugs of the nineteenth century: laudanum, an addictive form of opium that was used by people across social classes. The Stabler-Leadbeater Apothecary reminds us that the line between medicine and poison was sometimes a fine one. But as the Office of Historic Alexandria also interprets, things like arsenic, mercury, chloroform and strychnine all had a role to play in American medicine until medical practitioners began to realize that this kind of unregulated distribution needed oversight.

The interior of the Stabler-Leadbeater Apothecary.

The kinds of products found at the Stabler-Leadbeater Apothecary were as varied as the needs of any nineteenth-century household: products for cleaning, bug extermination, disease and illness and even for painting. E.S. Leadbeater was able to cash in on the many needs of a growing city like Alexandria, professionally serving customers with a trained staff and the help of his sons.

Gadsby's Tavern Museum
134 North Royal Street
Alexandria, VA 22314
www.gadsbystavern.org

In a way, Gadsby's Tavern set the stage for historic preservation and tourism in Alexandria in the pre–World War II world. In the 1920s and 1930s, the United States continued to feed its desire for the Colonial Revival, a style of architecture, furniture and much more that had permeated American culture since the 1876 centennial exposition in Philadelphia. The United

Left: The interior of the ballroom upstairs at Gadsby's Tavern Museum.

Below: The interior of the Gadsby's Tavern ballroom, which was removed from Alexandria and reinstalled at the Metropolitan Museum of Art in New York City. *Courtesy of the Metropolitan Museum of Art.*

States had survived one hundred years and a Civil War and had invested in this renewed story of nationhood by preserving stories in books and historic sites. No state was more heavily involved in this work than Virginia, the site of the first Revolutionary-era historic house preservation at Mount Vernon (you can read more about that in subsequent chapters) in the 1850s, Thomas Jefferson's Monticello in the 1920s and, finally, the ongoing work at Colonial Williamsburg, which was also begun in the 1920s. Gadsby's Tavern is Alexandria's version of this, which started the ball rolling for the town to revive itself, using Colonial Revival as its primary organizing vision.

First things first: as is often the case, preservation is spurred on by destruction of some sort. A curator from the Metropolitan Museum of Art (the Met) in New York paid a visit to Gadsby's Tavern in the early decades of the twentieth century and found an intact Georgian-decorated ballroom with hand-carved wooden dados and a gallery (balcony) for musicians. They purchased the room, removed it and sent the pieces north for installation in the Met. (In case you think this an amazing feat, don't forget that inside the Met is an Ancient Egyptian temple that was rebuilt block by block.) Today, this kind of purchase would be viewed as a form of cultural looting, no matter what the price. But at the time, Americans were the big buyers of the Western world, filling encyclopedic museums with art and artifacts from around the globe. The Metropolitan Museum of Art, arguably the country's most important art museum, uses the "Alexandria Ballroom" to display furniture, although in its time, the room would have been emptier, used as a flexible social gathering space. See www.metmuseum.org/about-the-met/curatorial-departments/the-american-wing/period-rooms/alexandria-ballroom for more information.

Gadsby's Tavern was then refurbished, and its historical associations became and remain important in the way Alexandria ties itself closely to George Washington and the colonial era. The tavern still hosts a "Birthnight Ball" for Washington every February; it's the centerpiece of an entire month of programs and activities honoring the first president. People wearing seventeenth-century costumes are not unusual sights in Alexandria (as in Williamsburg), especially when they are participating in the "country dances," which are offered at special times of the year. In addition, the tavern was the place of Thomas Jefferson's first presidential inaugural banquet. Located on a busy commercial corner, not far from the Potomac River and its wharves, Gadsby's Tavern was a locus for visitors, travelers, businesspeople and more for centuries. In the collection and on display are the portraits of Mr. and Mrs. John Gadsby, who were assisted in their work by those who never had

Patrons enjoying Gadsby's Tavern Restaurant.

their portraits painted: enslaved men and women who kept the many needs of the tavern users satisfied.

Next door to the historic, re-created tavern is a restaurant called, funnily enough, Gadsby's Tavern Restaurant. The restaurant is located inside one of the two buildings owned by John Gadsby, providing an authentic ambiance—the walls and floors are worn, the steps creak and the candles that are lit during the evening hours suggest conversations about politics from long ago. The food at Gadsby's Tavern Restaurant is a mix of traditional "Virginia fare," such as thick peanut soup, and lighter salads and sandwiches. Find the tavern's hours and menu here: www.gadsbystavernrestaurant.com.

HISTORIC ICE WELL AT GADSBY'S TAVERN

A final visit to Gadsby's Tavern reveals a unique vestige of the past: an underground icehouse, which the City of Alexandria cleverly opened for the public by creating a glass-walled enclosure to protect the site, but which allows for viewing. Stepping down into what is essentially a cellar on view,

Left: A re-created historic sign cut into stone, indicating the location of the historic ice well at Gadsby's Tavern.

Right: A marker in pavement where ice was lowered into the well at the corner of North Royal and Cameron Streets.

ice from the Potomac would be stored here for use during the warm weather months. A great reminder that refrigerators have been with us only for a short period of time. The icehouse seen here was in use for much longer.

Women's Suffrage Movement in Alexandria
Corner of South St. Asaph and Prince Streets
www.alexandriacelebrateswomen.com

There are many new sites to see in Virginia tied to the women's suffrage movement, which recently celebrated its centennial anniversary in August 2020. These new sites of commemoration include the Virginia Women's Monument in Richmond, the capital city, which showcases the story of many suffragists, and, of importance here, the Turning Point Suffragist Memorial, which is located in South Fairfax County and is described later in this book (page 177). But the City of Alexandria wanted to mark this occasion, too, and it did so by installing a new historic marker to remember the place where a customshouse once stood. Here, in a brick building that is now long gone, the Federal District Court of Alexandria was located on the third floor. This historic marker remembers the "infamous" Night of Terror, when thirty-two suffragists were arrested for picketing the White House—

the first group of Americans to ever do so. The women were divided up; some were taken to the Occoquan Workhouse in Lorton, where the women were brutalized and beaten, and others, including Lucy Burns, were force-fed. The plight of the women was leaked to the media, which spread their story far and wide, pressuring the authorities to relent. In the courthouse on the corner, the women were freed. A contemporary group of women called Alexandria Celebrates Women came together to document, commemorate and celebrate the lives and histories of many Alexandrian women over the ages—from the past to the present.

Old Presbyterian Meeting House
Tomb of the Unknown Soldier of the American Revolution
323 South Fairfax Street
Alexandria, VA 22314
www.opmh.org

Presbyterians in Alexandria have been worshipping together since 1760, but it wasn't until 1775 that the first building was erected on the site. This was the year of the "shot heard 'round the world" in Lexington and Concord, Massachusetts, which began the Revolutionary War. Seventy members of the congregation would fight in the American Revolution. In early 1800, the church hosted George Washington's memorial service—four times to accommodate numbers. In 1835, the wooden structure was gutted by fire, necessitating a new construction, but it was made to look old. Although it was Georgian in origin, the building's architectural style is called Reformed Protestant Plain style, and therefore, it appears unadorned when compared to other Christian churches in Alexandria.

It is essential to visit the burial ground behind the meetinghouse, as there are more than three hundred people interred here, including, most famously, an unknown soldier from the American Revolution. The Tomb of the Unknown Soldier of the American Revolution was established by the congregation when the remains of a man wearing a Revolutionary War uniform were exhumed from an earlier Catholic church and reburied in a special plot in 1826. Although people are familiar with the Daughters of the American Revolution (DAR), there are other associated groups doing similar work, including the National Society of the Children of the Revolution. This organization, still in existence and based in Washington, D.C., took on the project in the early twentieth century to create a memorial representing

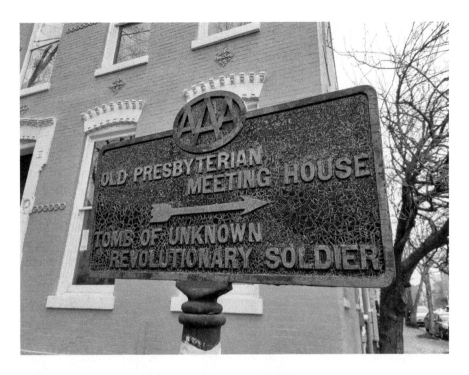

Above: A vintage AAA signage for the Old Presbyterian Meeting House and Tomb of the Unknown Revolutionary Soldier.

Left: The Old Presbyterian Meeting House's exterior (rear), showcasing "plain-style architecture" in the Reformed Protestant style.

A section of the *City Sweep* public art installation by Bernard Collin.

the more than 150,000 unidentified remains of Americans in the United States and abroad. The organization commissioned a marble "Epitaph to the Unknown Soldier," which reads:

> *Here lies a soldier of the Revolution whose identity is known but to God. His was an idealism that recognized a supreme being, that planted religious liberty on our shores, that overthrew despotism, that established a people's government, that wrote a Constitution setting metes and bounds of delegated authority, that fixed a standard of value upon above gold and lifted high the torch of civil liberty along the pathway of mankind. In ourselves, his soul exists as parts of ours, his memory's mansion.*

City Sweep
735 North St. Asaph Street
Alexandria, VA 22314
http://www.bernardcollin.com/project-for-old-town-alexandria-virginia.html

This triptych in cut metal depicts many identifiable and beloved parts and pieces of the city of Alexandria. Installed on an exterior brick wall near the grocery store Harris Teeter, the public artwork tells a story of Alexandria in precisely cut flat metal. Recognizable scenes include the Carlyle House, the hose pump at the Friendship Firehouse Museum, the Masonic symbol for the George Washington Masonic Memorial, boats on the Potomac River and more. French artist Bernard Collin was chosen to undertake this project and said of the work, "I opt only to use a hand-held plasma cutter. Having a computer duplicate my design is much too impersonal. It is important that every detail be my own, cut with precision and love. Each piece has its own personality." Harris Teeter is a good place to walk to for a cool drink and a sandwich. You can go across the street to eat and drink and stop for a moment to admire the triptych of the city's history displayed in metal.

Spite House
523 Queen Street
Alexandria, VA 22314

Measuring a whopping seven feet wide, the Spite House is Alexandria's smallest living space, and before the "tiny house movement" of the early twenty-first century, it was considered the smallest home in the United States. Sometimes called the "Queen Street Skinny House," the purpose of a house this size was to fill the space between already existing buildings. In this case, the house, which was built in 1830, was purposely built to keep people out of the alleyway, thus "spiting" those who would have used it to access places where they were not welcomed. The house is now privately owned.

Friendship Firehouse Museum
107 South Alfred Street
Alexandria, VA 22314
www.alexandria.gov/FriendshipFirehouse

Founded in 1774 as the Friendship Firehouse Company, Alexandria's active firefighting service has been in existence for more than 150 years. The substantial Friendship Firehouse is a two-story, Victorian-era brick construction with room on the ground level for firefighting apparatus and room on the second floor for meetings of a mutual aid— or fraternal-style society—elite men of Alexandria who recognized the value of maintaining an ever-professionalizing firefighting organization, a benefit to a community composed of mainly wooden buildings. George Washington was, not surprisingly, its leader, helping form the first volunteer firefighting society for Alexandria, as well as purchasing its first equipment. The Office of Historic Alexandria is currently conserving a fire hose reel. The hose reel is being restored to its original appearance which includes a dark-blue-and-gold paint scheme, different from the later, commonly recognized red-and-gold paint scheme. The second floor contains many evocative artifacts from the firehouse's early period, including a top hat painted with two hands clasped in a handshake under the word "Friendship." The mutual aid came not just from fighting fires but also in the form of payments to widows and families when volunteer firefighters died.

When walking the streets of Old Town, you easily notice the many painted plaques depicting "old-timey" firefighters and their hoses. While it might seem that these plaques indicated that an old house had fire insurance, these marked houses for "saving" should a fire break out. In fact, most of these plaques were put on houses during a high moment of the Colonial Revival, which brought a cultural taste for all things related to the founding fathers

Above: A second-floor meeting room of the Friendship Firehouse Museum.

Left: The Friendship Firehouse Museum's façade.

and colonial history. One tour leader pointed out that if a house was on fire and had no fire marker, the fire department would still come and assist—they would not have refused to fight a fire without a marker. As the Friendship Firehouse Museum notes, "Fire marks were used in some American cities, but they served as advertisements for the insurance companies and were a deterrent to arson."

Americans were heavily invested in the Colonial Revival, from its first appearance in 1876 during the centennial celebrations in Philadelphia to the bicentennial in 1976. Colonial Revival meant that Americans would build houses in a colonial style and/or decorate their interiors with colonial themes. Alexandria is a colonial city, but it is equally a Colonial Revival city— that is, the city purposefully highlighted elements of its colonial history and heritage. In the case of the firefighting plaques, which were installed in the 1930s and after, these markers harken back to the early days of firefighting and gave houses an identifiable mark of charm and taste for the Colonial Revival style.

Lee-Fendall House Museum and Garden

614 Oronoco Street
Alexandria, VA 22314
www.leefendallhouse.org

How do you know you're visiting a historic city? One answer: when you hear the news that a brick wall dating from the year 1800 or so has fallen and everyone is concerned. This happened to the Lee-Fendall House Museum on June 12, 2021, when, after a heavy rain, a seventy-foot-long portion of the red-brick wall delineating its garden fell into a heap. Historic architecture is a precious commodity in Alexandria; the city knows its value, and its value was built not only in the purpose it served but also in who made the walls, because, as in most parts of Virginia, bricks made before the Civil War were made by enslaved laborers. This gives the walls of houses, the walls around gardens and the sidewalks and streets a different aura once you realize that, while large kilns baked these bricks, human hands shaped them in molds and put them together, as the saying goes, brick by brick. After the collapse, the Lee-Fendall House Museum and Garden called in Alexandria's Board of Architectural Review and started a fundraising campaign to help offset the more than $125,000 cost to repair the sixty-ton Flemish-bond (a style of patterning) wall.

The dining table set for dinner at the Lee-Fendall House.

The Lee-Fendall House and Museum calls itself a "showcase of American history," as the house has a direct association with the Lee family of Virginia. General "Light Horse Harry" Lee, Robert E. Lee's father, owned this land before selling it to his cousin Philip Richard Fendall. Constructed in 1785 in a unique Maryland telescopic style, whereby each section of the house becomes smaller along an axis, the house looks as though it was built in stages. The first block of the house is the largest and is quite grand, but by the time you travel to the end, the construction is clearly informal and less expensive; these were quarters for the enslaved laborers of the house and their families, who lived there until the Civil War. A brick privy in the back is surrounded by what is today one of Alexandria's most historic and charming spots, especially if you like trees, flowers and shrubs (as apparently, many do). The trees in the attached garden are black walnuts, gingkos and magnolias, some with the respectable age of 150 years.

The house was later lived in by Robert Downham and then John L. Lewis; these men of the twentieth century and their families brought modern touches to the Federal-turned-Victorian house. But some of the original lifestyle remains intact and interpreted in spaces, such as the butler's pantry. On special Preservation Month (May) tours, visitors can see the array of bells still attached to their wires. This is especially interesting to think about when considering the professional work life of the last owner, John L. Lewis. As president of the United Mine Workers, Lewis was a well-known labor leader. A sitting room/office space on the second floor of the house is turned over to his story. Here, in this fashionably out-of-fashion wooden clapboard house, with a row of *Downton Abbey*–like bells, worked one of the most controversial and modern men of the twentieth century. Compare the Victorian Gothic chairs in the front hall with a modern chair that belonged to Lewis, and you get the juxtaposition and challenge of trying to do justice to the competing eras of the house's history.

Robert E. Lee's Boyhood Home
607 Oronoco Street
Alexandria, VA 22314

Here is a lesser-known story of the relationship between the family of George Washington and the Lees of Virginia. The second owner of the red-brick house was Colonel William Fitzhugh, a friend of Washington's. The close relationship between the two families is noted by the fact that only one month before he died, Washington dined here with the Fitzhughs. Later, the Lee family, headed by "Light Horse" Harry Lee and including his wife, Anne Hill Carter Lee, and five children, including Robert Edward Lee, rented the house, keeping it until 1825, the year young Robert E.

The Robert E. Lee Boyhood Home and Historic Marker (before removal).

Lee went to West Point and began down a path that would lead to infamy. The house is privately owned today and has recently been on the market. As one history guide noted, in Alexandria, Lee was surrounded by family members—his father left the family, but here, he had had uncles, aunts, cousins and a community.

4

GEORGE WASHINGTON AROUND ALEXANDRIA

George Washington's Townhouse
508 Cameron Street
Alexandria, VA 22314

One of the reasons Alexandria is called George Washington's hometown is its number of historic sites associated directly with the first president. Washington's original wood clapboard townhouse—rather unassuming to our modern eyes—provided him with a place to stay in the city while conducting business or a place to stopover when traveling. As a plantation owner involved with various enterprises, Washington depended on the accessibility of Alexandria to allow him to meet with others like him, attend to finances and banking, enjoy events at Gadsby's Tavern and participate as a member of the House of Burgesses. Although it is a private house today that is not open for visitors, it is worth the time to stroll by. A bust of Washington looks down at you from one of the windows, and the scale of the house presents a distinct difference to his main home, Mount Vernon. Behind the house is an alley called, of course, Washington Way. The original house was built between 1769 and 1771 and was torn down in 1855. The replica was created in 1960. The house has been passed between private hands—apparently, it was even rented for a while by Mick Fleetwood of Fleetwood Mac when he owned a club in Old Town—but you can stay here, too, if you'd like. The house is available for rent on Vrbo for $220 per night.

The exterior of the George Washington Townhouse, a twentieth-century replica of the original eighteenth-century building.

Christ Church

118 North Washington Street

Alexandria, VA 22314

www.HistoricChristChurch.org

Step inside the oversized metal gates that surround this parish church and sense a bit of spiritual life in eighteenth-century Alexandria. Although, today, it is located in a busy area of Old Town, where twenty-first-century traffic speeds by, and is surrounded by a lush, green lawn, strewn with old-style gravestones and memorials, Christ Church has been an important locale since 1767. The city—and the new country—grew up around it, and in this way, the church exists as witness to history. During the Civil War, the church was not adopted for use as a hospital like many churches in Alexandria were. Its historic nature and sanctity were kept intact, and U.S. Army chaplains led services there. Surely, this was one of the reasons why visitors, such as Winston Churchill and Franklin Delano Roosevelt, came to the church

The exterior of Christ Church, located in what was once the edge of town.

during World War II. A sense of continuity in difficult times can be found in a place like Christ Church.

Due to its inception during the Georgian period—with architecture designed in a Classical flavor and named for King George III of England—the Flemish-bond brick building has Aquia quoins at each end, with Palladian windows that illuminate the pulpit and altar area inside. You will see references to Aquia sandstone regularly if you become a student of architecture in the DMV (District of Columbia-Maryland-Virginia), as many eighteenth- and nineteenth-century buildings, including, most famously, the White House and the U.S. Capitol, were built with Aquia sandstone. This particular sandstone was quarried in Stafford County in Northern Virginia and was well regarded for its ease of carving, although this also meant it was rather porous and susceptible to the elements. George Washington, Christ Church's most famous parishioner, used Aquia as a building material, but it was also used for steps, fireplace surrounds and cornerstones.

The Washington family pew box still exists at Christ Church (on the left side, toward the front, if one is facing the pulpit). Washington was already a member of the Truro Parish in South Fairfax County, but he attended services at Christ Church as well when he was in Alexandria for business, staying at his townhouse on 508 Cameron Street. A Washington relative by marriage, Robert E. Lee, was baptized here in 1853 and regularly attended services.

Although the interior is plain, with little decoration beyond the hand-lettered wall panels with the Ten Commandments and a series of memorials on the lower walls, the exterior of Christ Church offers much more. Until 1809, the churchyard was the original burying ground for Alexandria and is filled with interesting and historic gravestones. It's fun to try to decipher gravestones and appreciate their historic sculpture and early carvings. In the churchyard is a unique memorial called the "Confederate Mound." A spot of earth, with daffodils pushing up around it, sits close to the North Washington Street fence. An inscribed marble tablet records the place of burial for members of the Confederate States of America (CSA). Another monument worthy of attention is the Charles Bennett Memorial. Designed by Robert Mills, the original architect of the Washington Monument, this smaller-scaled obelisk notes that Bennett died in "Alexandria, D.C.," indicating the city was still part of the capital city at the time of Bennett's death and burial. Finally, Christ Church is one of the best places to enjoy native trees. In the churchyard are southern magnolias, willows, white and

Confederate Soldiers Burial Mound, Christ Church.

English oaks, horse chestnuts, American hollies and dogwoods—a verdant landscape for the dead to rest in and for the living to visit.

Plaque for the Homesite of Dr. James Craik

210 Duke Street
Alexandria, VA

One name of a second-tier "important man" that appears in Alexandria is that of Dr. James Craik. Craik was one of the doctors who attended George Washington in his last illness in 1799. He was born around the same time as Washington, served as surgeon in Braddock's campaign and was with Washington throughout the Revolutionary War. Second-tier historical figures often get lost when standing beside their more famous contemporaries, but Craik has a special place in the history of Alexandria and in the city's landscape. His upright and substantial grave marker can be seen in the Old Presbyterian Meeting House Graveyard, along the pathway to the right of the meeting house.

Left: A plaque for the homesite of Dr. James Craik.

Right: The gravestone of Dr. James Craik at the Old Presbyterian Meeting House Graveyard.

George Washington Bench
Duvall House
305 Cameron Street
Alexandria, VA 22314

This unusual bronze monument of Washington at rest was placed at the front-facing façade of the Duvall House, which was once a tavern. A large gathering of Alexandrians came together when Washington announced his resignation as commander-in-chief of the army after the Revolutionary War had ended. A thirteen-cannon salute was given to Washington, fired from Market Square. Although Duvall House was the scene of Washington's life as a seasoned and triumphant adult, the sculpture commissioned shows a youthful Lieutenant Colonel George Washington, thoughtful and perhaps a bit resigned. This is due to his role in the march of Colonel Braddock's army from the Carlyle House and Alexandria through the Ohio Valley to try to wrestle Fort Duquesne from the French. The military expedition was a failure, and Braddock himself died and was buried along the army's route back. Braddock Road in Alexandria, Fairfax County, was named for Washington's commander. Thus, Duvall House is a place to remember the bookend events in the military life of the first president.

George Washington in bronze, sitting on a bench in front of historic Duvall House.

A small plaster bust peeks out of a high window to the right of the front door, and a "Don't Tread on Me" flag is often seen flying. Due to its historic association with local and national history, Duvall House was landmarked; the site was also the location of the first bank in Alexandria and, much later, the dressmaker Frankie Welch, who dressed women of the mid-twentieth century, including Lady Bird Johnson and Betty Ford. If you are visiting Alexandria, you might want to stay here. Today, the brick building is available on AirBnB as a short-term rental and on HomeAway/Vrbo.

George Washington Masonic National Memorial
101 Callahan Drive
Alexandria, VA 22301
www.gwmemorial.org

On February 20, 2023, not too far into the future at the time of this book's publication, the George Washington Masonic National Memorial will commemorate its centennial by reenacting the original laying of its cornerstone. Memorials and monuments are in the news quite a bit these days, and it would be hard to try to ignore this one—the memorial is the defining element of the Alexandria skyline, rising 333 feet above Old Town.

Masons and Freemasonry retain an aura of mystery due to the secretive nature of their ancient practices. The Masons themselves say they have "done more for the world in which we live than most people—even Masons—realize." Beginning in medieval Europe as a fraternity of stone masons, these local organizations of working men grew in number and presence throughout the Age of Enlightenment, transforming themselves from a hands-on, laboring society to an attractive cultural platform of self-governing, in which men like "Brother George Washington," "Brother Benjamin Franklin" and many other American Revolutionaries would be exposed to democracy (Masonic lodges created their own bylaws and elected their own leaders). Although women were never accepted as Masons, Black men saw the value of such local, formal societies, and in places like Alexandria, they formed their own lodges. Alexandria's Universal Lodge No. 1, Virginia's first "Prince Hall," was formed in 1845.

The Alexandria Lodge is a palpable symbol of the power the Freemasons had by the early twentieth century. And there is no more powerful figure representative of Freemasonry in the United States than George Washington. The architecture selected for the memorial, which is also a museum, is a tower of descending blocks—something akin to a ziggurat in ancient Mesopotamia or a step pyramid in ancient Egypt. Outside, the memorial tower, with a light at its pinnacle, is surrounded by a thirty-seven-acre park, through which visitors can drive on a winding road designed by the Olmsted Brothers Firm. Inside, visitors are faced with oversized everything. When walking between massive columns to the portal (or grand doorway), one can see Washington in bronze rising from his chair, his robust physique a reminder of the emphasis Washington placed on his own physicality and on the interplay between the old stone masons—men who labored in stone—and the new, who focused on a balance between body, faith and mind.

Standing on the steps of the George Washington National Masonic Memorial, overlooking the city of Alexandria and Washington, D.C.

Beyond Memorial Hall are a series of rooms, small and large, in which museum exhibits displaying authentic Masonic artifacts, such as a room recreated as a 1794 lodge, complete with spittoons next to each seat, can be seen. There is a theater and more lodges for current meetings within

The front exterior of the George Washington Masonic Memorial. *Courtesy Joe Ravi, CC BY-SA 3.0, via Wikimedia Commons, www. creativecommons.org.*

the building. George Washington is seen in multiple exhibits throughout the memorial and in a series of murals painted in several spaces throughout the building. A chapel and an observation deck look out over Alexandria; Washington, D.C.; and the Potomac River. The George Washington Masonic Memorial achieved National Historic Landmark status in 2015.

Alexandria War Dead Memorial
Alexandria Union Station
110 Callahan Drive
Alexandria, VA 22301

This historic memorial, dwarfed by the tower of the George Washington Masonic National Memorial across the busy street, sits quietly in a highly trafficked parking area at Alexandria's Union Station, the passenger train station for Amtrak. The memorial was dedicated at the start of World War II to remember the war dead from Alexandria in World War I. Community

Alexandria War Dead Memorial.

war memorials were often commissioned by veterans' groups, as was the case of the Alexandria War Dead Memorial, which was commissioned by Russell Mitchel Post 609 of the Veterans of Foreign Wars (VFW) and the Citizens of Alexandria. The project was paid for by Florence Angelo Cannaday from Richmond, Virginia. The structure of the memorial is stark: a thick cylinder of polished granite rises twenty-two feet, with a stepped pattern pushing up a cross at the top. It's hard not to see a relationship between the stepping of the stone at the memorial's apex with the stepped-tier structure of the Masonic memorial close by, which predates this World War I memorial.

To complete the theme of memorials to the war dead of Alexandria, one should also see the World War II Memorial on the grounds of George Washington Middle School at 1005 Mount Vernon Avenue. Although it is much smaller than the World War I memorial, this obelisk of rough-hewn granite contains more names, indicating how much longer this war was for Americans. The memorial was "dedicated to the memory of our boys who served in World War II and did not come back."

5

WATERFRONT AND MARITIME HISTORY

Captain's Row
100 Block of Prince Street
Alexandria, VA 22314

One of the most photographed spots in Alexandria, Captain's Row, is one of the city's few remaining original cobblestone streets. The homes lining each side of the street are mostly from the eighteenth century, and many were built by Captain John Harper for the city's growing merchant class. The cobblestones may have been sourced from the many ships that were coming into port, where they were used as ballast. They were perhaps originally pulled from local rivers, where rushing waters smoothed their surfaces over time. Cobblestone street paving was first developed by the ancient Romans, then revived in England and eventually used in the English colonies (Boston, for example, has a few remaining cobblestone streets in Beacon Hill). Cobblestone streets were laid out by hand and were easy on horses' hooves while never developing ruts, all useful qualities.

In Alexandria, a tree canopy arches over Prince Street's cobblestones, and many residents sustain charming miniature gardens around their doorways and windows. Farther afield, Alexandria's houses become more varied architecturally and larger, but streets like these are rare, authentic and picturesque, beloved by residents and visitors alike. Captain's Row has recently been in the news, due to the growing traffic in Old Town, especially when lower King Street was closed in 2020–21 during the pandemic and then changed permanently into a pedestrian-only thoroughfare. This put

Captain's Row, an original cobblestone street in Old Town.

added pressure on an already overused historic road surface, asking the question: how does a historic city continue to develop while preserving its past? There are a few other cobblestone streets and alleys in Old Town.

Tall Ship *Providence*
1 Cameron Street, Lower Level
Alexandria, VA 22314
www.tallshipprovidence.org

The tall ship *Providence* is one of the newer historical attractions at Waterfront Park and lends a decidedly authentic nautical air to the scene. The idea behind bringing a re-created tall ship to the Alexandria Waterfront was

An interpreter explaining the significance of the ship *Providence* before boarding for tour.

to provide a step back in time to the eighteenth century, when ships of various sizes and scales plied the Atlantic Ocean, entering the Chesapeake Bay and sailing up to Alexandria. The background story of the original sloop *Providence*, built in Rhode Island in the 1760s, and its later re-creation for the bicentennial in 1976, is nothing short of a miracle that the ship exists at all today. In its first life as a Providence, Rhode Island–built sloop, the *Katy* served as a merchant/whaling/privateering ship. With the start of the Revolutionary War, the *Katy* was adopted by the Continental Congress as one of the first ships in the new navy and rechristened the *Providence*. John Paul Jones took on the role of captain of *Providence* in 1776, noted as being his favorite command. The ship and its captains served well, capturing "prizes" (other ships filled with valuable goods) until 1779, when the *Providence* was caught with other American ships by the British navy in what is today Maine. Instead of allowing the ships to fall into British hands, the *Providence* and the others were burned.

So, the *Providence* went to its watery grave off the coast of Maine, and almost two hundred years later, an American named John Fitzhugh Millar began building a new *Providence* for the country's bicentennial celebrations in 1976. If you are familiar with the trials and tribulations of building and/or owning a boat of any size, you'll already know what is coming. The *Providence* was rebuilt and sailed for many years, but eventually, the cost of maintaining a vessel of this size overwhelmed the first foundation, and from there, the *Providence* went through a series of owners, disasters and even a two-time stint in the *Pirates of the Caribbean* franchise films. Purchased by the Tall Ship *Providence* Foundation in Alexandria, the *Providence* was restored and given a new lease on life, sailing the Potomac beginning in 2019.

The organization runs public and private tours guided by costumed interpreters who tell stories centered on the life of Captain John Paul Jones and the sailors of the Continental navy. Jones was Scottish but rose through the ranks to become commander of the first American navy. If you visit George Washington's Mount Vernon, you will see a bust of Jones that is placed directly over the rear door to Washington's private study, alluding to Washington's desire to join the navy, not the army, as a young man. You can take tall ship *Providence* out for a private charter or attend a public sail. Located close by on the wharf are several boating excursion companies, including the Potomac Riverboat Company.

Torpedo Factory Art Center
105 North Union Street
Alexandria, VA 22314
www.torpedofactory.org

Today, the Torpedo Factory Art Center is filled with 160 working artists spread throughout three levels, with 82 open studios and an art supply store. Rewind the clock more than one hundred years, and the building, first opened in 1919, was churning out munitions for World War I and II. Functioning for only two years, the torpedo factory had a segregated workforce, and Black men did most of the dangerous work. Many Black people migrated north to work in such plants in the early twentieth century

The exterior of the Torpedo Art Factory.

and would do so in greater numbers as the century wore on. The factory went offline after World War I, but after a quiet period between the wars, it was reactivated in 1937 and named the Navy Torpedo Station. Here, in historic Alexandria, directly on the Potomac Waterfront, 9,920 torpedoes were made by an integrated workforce—including women—before World War II ended in 1945.

Economic and community developers saw an opportunity to reuse industrial spaces beginning in the 1970s, when many of them had been abandoned in cities across the nation. The torpedo factory became a gallery and working space for artists in 1974 and has been open ever since (close to fifty years of art in place of munitions). Its genres of art-making include ceramics, fiber, jewelry, printmaking, photography and sculpture, among others. The Alexandria Art League also functions out of the Torpedo Factory Art Center, organizing art classes and exhibits for the community. Unfortunately, like many not-for-profit arts organizations, the Torpedo Factory Art Center, which is central to the Old Town experience, opening its to doors to residents and visitors far and wide, has experienced decades' worth of financial difficulties. Currently, there is a group working to determine its future, as the push-pull between the arts and economics, always a struggle in the United States, plays out in the historic space on Alexandria's Waterfront.

Alexandria Archaeology Museum
105 North Union Street, no. 327
Torpedo Factory
Alexandria, VA 22314
www.alexandria.gov/Archaeology

The City of Alexandria can boast of many things, and archaeology is surely one of them. Alexandria has one of the largest collections of archaeological material in the country, much of which was excavated during the urban renewal of the 1970s, a period when many historic buildings were torn down to make way for modern structures. This archaeological record is under continual study and has become especially valuable in establishing more knowledge of the city's maritime and Black history. Alexandria had one of the largest Black populations in the country and is currently undertaking archaeological work to learn more about the city's free Black community and the ways in which they moved around the city, following social and economic opportunities and challenges.

Above: The Alexandria Archaeology Museum, part of the City of Alexandria, has its public-facing space located inside the Torpedo Factory Art Center on the second floor.

Right: An archaeology display showing glass and ceramics from Arell's Tavern site, circa 1760s.

Today, traditional methods of archaeology, such as digging test pits and excavating and documenting one-by-one-foot squares, are supplemented with digital technologies, which have transformed what we can learn from the past. In 2005, for example, Alexandria Archaeology partnered with the Center for Geospatial Information Technology at Virginia Tech to create the Alexandria Archaeology Digital Atlas. Since that time, the information available on the digital mapping project continues to grow, offering both researchers and the public new ways to find buried information. Learn more at www.alexandriava.gov/historic/archaeology/default.aspx?id=39058.

The *Shipbuilder* Monument
SE Corner of Waterfront Park
1A Prince Street
Alexandria, VA 22314

Standing strong against the sea, the *Shipbuilder* pays tribute to Alexandria's maritime heritage, which is evident throughout the city, particularly in Waterfront Park. Drawing residents and visitors alike, especially on the weekends, Waterfront Park is situated on land that was built on pilings and fill, some of which happens to be ships. In addition to the *Shipbuilder* monument, Waterfront Park has become the site of a changing public art space for the city. The series, called *Site See: New Views in Old Town*, was started in 2019. In 2020, the well-regarded *Wrought, Knit, Labors, Legacy* installation by Olalekan Jeyifous featured oversized Black figures with painted-on compass patterns facing the Potomac River. This work was so popular that the City of Alexandria asked the artist if the works could be kept and displayed elsewhere. Four of the figures were moved to a local community center. Continuing the maritime theme, in 2021, the work of art was called *Groundswell* and featured a landscape of wooden pilings of different sizes, pushing the coastline of Alexandria farther out into the Potomac. Created by Mark Reigelman, the pilings were of varying heights and featured a watery, blue surface on the top, with wavy lines reminding viewers of the rings of trees and the passage of time. *Groundswell* garnered much attention, mostly from families who hang out on and near the sculpture, kids standing on the pilings and posing for photographs. The *Shipbuilder*, alas, gets much less attention—let's give him some.

Created by Michael Curtis in 2004, the lone figure of a man wearing a long coat stands against the wind, the sea lapping against his lower legs.

Right: The *Shipbuilder* Monument on the Potomac River Waterfront in Alexandria.

Below: A propeller from a World War II submarine on the waterfront, the tall ship *Providence* in the background.

Classical scrolls complement his marble base. In his right hand are tools of the trade. Other maritime-themed memorials and public art installations, including a massive propeller or "screw" from a World War II submarine and the public boat facilities run by the Alexandria Seaport Foundation, can be found as you walk along the series of waterfront parks in Alexandria.

Flounder Houses
Various locations in Alexandria

A unique architectural house form can be found along the waterfront and in several places in Old Town. Called "flounder houses," these narrow, vertical, brick, three-story buildings have sloped roofs and no windows on one side— much like a flat flounder skimming across the ocean floor. There are two flounder houses that are fun to see, and both are located in alleyways with cobblestone streets: one is right around the corner from the Carlyle House in Ramsay Alley and the other is in Wales Alley on Lee Street. A third easy-to-identify flounder house exists as part of the Old Presbyterian Meeting House property. You know it's a flounder house because the sign over the front door reads, "316–Flounder House." This is the oldest known flounder house in Alexandria, dating from 1787. Its original use was as a parsonage for the minister and his family.

Plinth
The Gables
525 Montgomery Street
Alexandria, VA 22314

This work of public art is dedicated to a historic transportation route that was eventually buried: the Alexandria Canal, a different kind of waterfront. The canal was built to connect the trade in Alexandria and from interior Virginia to the C&O Canal, which traversed 185 miles from Georgetown (Washington, D.C.) to Cumberland, Maryland. The eighteen-foot-tall *Plinth* was designed by artist Tom Fruin and installed in 2019, a successful example of the relationship between public art and placemaking for development. A coffeehouse is located near *Plinth*, and its patrons sit around the colorful stained glass–like installation during warm weather. The Alexandria Canal ran close by on Montgomery Street. The artwork is an abstract representation

An example of a "flounder house" in Alexandria's Ramsay Alley.

of a somewhat forgotten part of Alexandrian history, but its linear/vertical orientation reminds viewers of a map. The first part of the C&O Canal along Constitution Avenue and the National Mall is also now buried and gone, thus artworks like this can serve several purposes: a sign marker for people to locate themselves and other places, a teaching tool for people to remember the past and a visual artwork that is interesting in and of itself to experience and enjoy.

Promenade Classique
Tide Lock Park
1 Canal Center Plaza
Alexandria, VA 22314

This work of public art is a bit unusual for Alexandria, a city that prides itself on its traditional, Colonial Revival–style aesthetics and history. The *Promenade Classique* is an oversized installation spread over multiple areas of a development called Canal Center that was planned in the 1980s. You remember big hair, right? This is the same thing, just in public art. The site, located on a small bluff overlooking the Potomac River and basically right on/over the historic Alexandria Canal, was redeveloped by a firm that saw an opportunity to make a splash with art, so to speak. A collective from the Washington, D.C. art museum community was assembled to visit the site and make suggestions, which included installing a re-created lock to represent the canal. Winning the commission with their proposal for marble monuments in pieces was the French husband-and-wife artist team of Anne and Patrick Poirier, alongside landscape architect M. Paul Friedberg.

From one level to the next, water is the piece's theme, and it allows for reflection and a place to congregate in the otherwise stale, corporate courtyard space. When walking down the staircase, viewers find themselves near colossal pieces of "marble" statuary. Do the oversized eyes and mouths of the colossus make you think of the ancient world? Is this a reference to the ancient city of Alexandria in Egypt, which once held a lighthouse and the world's largest library? Like with many works of public art, the meaning behind *Promenade Classique* is open to interpretation. But when standing near the base of the miniature obelisk and looking out over the Potomac River, toward the Washington Monument and Washington, D.C., the connection between these two places, which have a long, shared history, is undeniable. Turning away

Above: A re-created
Alexandria canal lock.

Right: Part of the *Promenade
Classique* public art
installation.

from the overblown architectural and artistic structure behind you, from the Alexandria side, standing along the water's edge, perhaps at sunset, you might think about just how lucky you are to be there.

Jones Point Park
125 Jones Point Drive
Alexandria, VA 23242
www.nps.gov/gwmp/planyourvisit/jonespoint

Jones Point Park is a huge draw for Alexandrians and the visitors who discover this sweet spot, where the Potomac River winds its way out to the Chesapeake Bay. Jones Point Park is a little bit of everything: a multiuse recreational green space with basketball courts and a playground, a returned-to-naturalized landscape meant to support insects and bird life with a long history to boot. At Jones Point Park, you are just as likely to find community gardeners, dog walkers and birdwatchers with their binoculars as you are to find bikers, joggers and fishermen. But the park was once home to a massive shipyard during World War I, remnants of which you can identify with help from historical signage. These remnants include a massive wooden ship rudder and the concrete tracks that were used to pull ships in and out of the water. Between the wars, Jones Point Park had a Civilian Conservation Corps (CCC) camp that employed men to improve the area by tearing down abandoned buildings and constructing roads.

Furthermore, Jones Point Park has an even more robust historical pedigree: the city's last riverside lighthouse is located here, which had a Fresnel lens set into the roofline of a wooden, white-painted clapboard house. The lighthouse operated from 1855 to 1926, and two of the original lights were refurbished and can be seen on display at the Alexandria History Museum at the Lyceum. Stop for a moment to think how these beautiful, massive glass objects must have been a welcome sight when sailing in darkness.

But you are not done yet. Located next to the lightkeepers' house is the original 1791 southern cornerstone boundary marker, dating to the era when Alexandria was part of Washington, D.C. The very end of the corner of this part of the "D.C. Diamond" was placed here, laid out by learned men under the guidance of city plan designer Pierre L'Enfant and surveyor Andrew Ellicott. The entire boundary was marked with engraved stones placed a mile apart from each other. Benjamin Banneker was one of those who was chosen to be a part of Ellicott's team, selected for his skills in mathematics

Jones Point Park with one of the D.C.-Virginia-Maryland boundary markers. In the background is the last remaining riverine lighthouse on the Potomac River.

and astronomy. Called the "first Black man of science," Banneker also was the first to study cicadas—this must be noted, as in 2021, when this book was being written, a seventeen-year cicada bloom (called Brood X) occurred. The stone was set into the ground as part of the retaining or seawall and is now covered with plexiglass, but the National Park Service has installed modern boundary markers nearby, noting where Virginia; Washington, D.C.; and Maryland all met on a spit of land jutting into the river. The commemorative plaque, with a passage from the April 15, 1791 placement for the cornerstone, reads:

> *May this stone long commemorate the goodness of God*
> *In those uncommon events which have given America a name among nations—*
> *Under this stone, may jealousy and selfishness be forever buried!*

This is great history, but it is hardly complete without mentioning the first person who owned this land, a woman who lived in the seventeenth century and received a land patent directly from the Colony of Virginia. A woman in a position of power in the early modern period was rare enough, and Margaret Brent was a singular figure. As noted on the wayfinding signage that was provided by the National Park Service (and close to one of the boundary markers), Brent was able to own land because she was not married, but she was also a vocal advocate for women's rights, asking for the right to vote from the Maryland legislature when she and her sister moved there for freedom. This right was not granted, and Brent left Maryland for Virginia, where she purchased around ten thousand acres along the Potomac River in what is now Fairfax County. A portion of the land she once owned became Old Town in Alexandria, but she is remembered one mile away in Jones Point Park with a bronze plaque that was installed by the Daughters of the American Revolution (DAR). In 1978, the DAR called her an "extraordinary woman" for her efforts in fighting gender discrimination in a patriarchal society. She died in 1671, and a bronze plaque dedicated to her also exists in the Maryland State Capitol Building.

Jones Point Park is located on the Mount Vernon Trail, which connects Arlington and Alexandria to Mount Vernon, so this is a busy spot for visitors, especially on the weekends. The parking lot is small and always full. Walk or ride your bike in, either on the paved trail or on the road (closed to moving traffic) directly under the Woodrow Wilson Bridge. This massive bridge was built in 1961, eight years after the City of Alexandria voted for the construction of the $20 million project. The bridge spans the Potomac River, connecting Alexandria to National Harbor.

6
BLACK HISTORY AND HERITAGE

Alfred Street Baptist Church
301 South Alfred Street
Alexandria, VA 22314
www.alfredstreet.org

From the historic marker in front of the church, the long and illustrious history of the congregation—the people—of Alfred Street Baptist Church comes into view:

> *Alfred Street Baptist Church is home to the oldest African American congregation in Alexandria, dating to the early 19th century. It has served as a prominent religious, educational, and cultural institution. In 1818, the congregation, then known as the Colored Baptist Society, began worship services here in the midst of the Bottoms, a free Black neighborhood. By 1820, the church created its educational branch, providing religious and secular opportunities for both Black children and adults. In 1855, free Black craftsmen probably designed and built the brick church. Alterations to the building occurred in the 1880s, and in 1994, the church created a new sanctuary.*

Above: Alfred Street Baptist Church.

Opposite: The reverse of the Edmonson Sisters Monument, showing the ship *The Pearl*, on which the Edmonson sisters made their daring escape.

Edmonson Sisters Monument
1701 Duke Street
Alexandria, VA 22314

One of Alexandria's permanent and newer public monuments that tells an inspiring story from history is this huge block of bronze, from which two women move out of the past and into the present. And it is located where we met them on their journey. Mary and Emily Edmonson were enslaved young women in Washington, D.C. In 1848, they and seventy-five other Black Americans escaped aboard the schooner *The Pearl*, which is depicted on the back of the monument. The ship was captured, and the sisters were sold to Joseph Bruin, who placed them in the Bruin or "Negro Jail" in Alexandria. Abolitionists were often activists, and some, like Reverend Henry Ward Beecher, used such events to raise awareness of the plight of not only the Edmonson sisters but also all enslaved Black people. Raising

awareness is one thing, but Beecher also helped raise funds so that, with Paul Edmonson, the father of the young women, Mary and Emily gained their freedom. Beecher was part of a family who were made famous by their abolitionist activities, recognizable across the country due to the book *Uncle Tom's Cabin*, which was written by Beecher's sister Harriet Beecher

Stowe. The Edmonson sisters went on to join the abolitionist community and attend Oberlin College. There is a plaque at 1707 Duke Street to note where the original Bruin Jail was once located.

L'Ouverture Hospital
Prince Street and 217–19 South Payne Street
Alexandria, VA 22314

There is both a Virginia Department of Historic Resources Marker here and a much longer privately installed marker on the exterior of this blue-painted brick rowhouse. The overview of the site reads:

> *Named for Toussaint L'Ouverture, the Haitian revolutionary. L'Ouverture Hospital opened early in 1864 near the freedmen's barracks in Alexandria to serve sick and injured United States Colored Troops (USCT). Designed by the U.S. Army, the hospital complex could accommodate about 700 patients and occupied the city block just south of here. The hospital also served African American civilians, many of whom had escaped from slavery and sought refuge in Alexandria. In Dec. 1864, more than 400 patients led a successful protest demanding that USCTs be buried in Alexandria National Cemetery, with full honors, rather than at the Contrabands and Freedmen Cemetery.*

Filling out the story of the hospital, the second, longer marker tells us that 217 South Payne Street was originally surrounded by twelve or more buildings and tents for patients. The area was, in fact, a large ad hoc hospital complex with a "surgeon's dispensary, cook house, linen room, heating plant, sutlers' quarters, schoolhouse and 'dead house.'" In other words, it was a small city within a city and 217 South Payne Street, which served as hospital headquarters, is the only surviving structure from that era. The sign further tells us that Private John Cooley, a soldier of the Twenty-Seventh U.S. Colored Infantry from Ohio was the first Black soldier to die in Alexandria, "[who] died upon entering L'Overture Hospital on May 4, 1864."

On walking tours of Alexandria, you are also likely to hear about one doctor, due to some unusual circumstances that surrounded him. On May 17, 1864, Dr. William C. Minor, a surgeon captain, began working a L'Ouverture Hospital. He later murdered an individual in England, and on April 6, 1872, Minor was found not guilty of murder after it was said that he was a "certified

L'Ouverture Hospital
Office (now a private
home).

lunatic." He was, however, held in permanent custody. While in custody, Dr. Minor became a core creator of the *Oxford English Dictionary*, submitting over ten thousand definitions. This part of the story of Dr. Minor was recounted in the 1998 Simon Winchester book *The Professor and the Madman*, which later became a film starring Mel Gibson and Sean Penn.

This site is connected to the Contrabands and Freedmen Cemetery and to the Alexandria National Cemetery. Many of the patients who died at L'Ouverture were buried in the Contrabands and Freedmen Cemetery, including Black soldiers, who stated, "We are now sharing equally the dangers and hardships in this mighty contest and should shair [*sic*] the same privileges and rights of burial in every way with our fellow soldiers who differ only in color." Afterward, soldiers were interred in the Alexandria National Cemetery. This petition, signed by more than 400 people out of the more than 1,400 who were admitted here as patients, is an example of the many ways in which Alexandria played a role in advancing the civil rights movement.

Freedom House Museum
Franklin & Armfield Slave Trading Post
1315 Duke Street
Alexandria, VA 22314
www.alexandriava.gov/FreedomHouse

Called "ground zero" of the domestic slave trade in the Chesapeake region by the Office of Historic Alexandria, the city recently raised more than $17,000 from the public to go toward new exhibits for the three-story interior of Freedom House. The Office of Historic Alexandria intends to use the space to not only tell the story recounted by Joshua Rothman in his *The Ledger and the Chain: How Domestic Slave Traders Shaped America* (New York: Basic Books, 2021) but also relate the larger story of Black Americans in Alexandria. In addition to new exhibits, new, equitable amenities and systems upgrades, including a new HVAC system, ADA-compliant bathrooms and an elevator, are being installed in the museum, and they may be open by the time you are reading this book.

Rothman's book provides a thorough documentation of the years between 1828 and 1836, when business partners Isaac Franklin, John Armfield and, later, Rice Ballard built up a business in the slave trade, benefitting from a moment in time when Virginia was purging itself of enslaved people due to the downturn in tobacco growing. At the same time, the need for enslaved people in the lower southern states was growing exponentially due to the use of the cotton gin. Rothman spoke about his book during one of 2021's many Zoom talks, setting the stage for the role of slavery in the young United States. The institution of slavery was intrinsic to the development of the nation, and the slave trade, or the trade of humans, had "a birth and death, a rhythm, and a cycle." Franklin & Armfield established much of this movement, forcing more than ten thousand people to the Deep South, one of the largest forced migrations in American history. And a forced migration it was, as humans were chained together in a "coffle" (a long line) and literally marched southward.

But on Duke Street, the façade of the Franklin & Armfield building displayed a refined antebellum elegance in its front rooms—a strategy used by the slave traders to demonstrate the validity of the slave trade against antislavery advocates and abolitionists. Meanwhile, the backyard held literal pens, much like animal pens or enclosures. Slave trade advertisements were seen in all the local newspapers, and Rothman tracked down Franklin's very first slave trade advertisement in the *Alexandria Phoenix Gazette*, a paper that

The annual Scottish Christmas Walk in Alexandria, celebrating the city's Scottish heritage.

The exterior of the Alexandria Visitor Center, located inside the historic Ramsay House.

The interior of Carlyle House, showing the room dedicated to Colonel Edward Braddock and his ill-fated military expedition in March 1755 against the French at Fort Duquesne. George Washington was a member of the local militia in this effort. Braddock was shot, killed and buried on the route back.

An earthenware vessel with a slip, circa the 1790s, made by Henry Piercy, the first ceramicist in Alexandria. Piercy ran a pottery and retail shop. This vessel is now on display in the Alexandria History Museum at the Lyceum.

The exterior of the Lee-Fendell House, showing Maryland telescoping style.

The interior of the Stabler-Leadbeater Apothecary.

The exterior of the Athenaeum.

The interior of Gadsby's Tavern Museum.

Top: The graveyard of the Old Presbyterian Meeting House. The Tomb of the Unknown Soldier of the American Revolution can be seen in the back of the photograph on the far right.

Bottom: *City Sweep*, by Bernard Collin, a public art installation at 500 Madison Street.

Above: The exterior of the Murray-Dick-Fawcett House, considered the oldest and most intact historic house in Alexandria.

Left: The famous "Spite House" or "Skinny House" of Queen Street, Alexandria.

The Friendship Firehouse Museum.

Fire markers for buildings can be found around Old Town, suggesting colonial dates, but they were installed in the twentieth century for "period detail."

Right: A colossal bronze statue of the first president inside the George Washington National Masonic Memorial.

Below: The interior of the *Providence*, with a John Paul Jones reenactor.

Above: The interior of the Torpedo Art Factory with an authentic artifact in the lobby.

Left: *Plinth*, by Tom Fruin (2019), which is used to mark the site of the buried Alexandria Canal.

Left: The Edmonson
Sisters Monument.

Below: Public art and
memorial installations
at the Contraband and
Freedmen's Cemetery.

Right: The public art installation at the African American Heritage Memorial Park in the Carlyle section of Alexandria.

Below: The Fort Ward Historic Site.

Left: The "Witness Tree," planted at Fort Hunt by King George of England during World War II.

Below: The exterior of George Washington's Mount Vernon.

A re-created slave cabin at the Pioneer Farmer Site at George Washington's Mount Vernon.

The interior of the Pope-Leighey House, designed by Frank Lloyd Wright and owned by the National Trust for Historic Preservation.

The exterior of the U.S. Army Museum at Fort Belvoir.

The exterior of Historic Huntley, owned by Fairfax County and run by a partnership between the Parks and Recreation Department and Friends of Historic Huntley.

Above: The "Chinoiserie" Room at Gunston Hall.

Right: The interior of the Lucy Burns Museum, part of the Workhouse Arts Center in Lorton.

The interior of the beehive kiln, part of the original Occoquan Workhouse, located today at Occoquan Regional Park.

Suffragist Mary Church Terrell, a cofounder of the NAACP and a professor, in bronze, part of the Turning Point Memorial at Occoquan Regional Park.

Left: Freedom House Museum of the City of Alexandria. Closed for renovation.

Right: Alexandria, Virginia. Slave Pen, Interior View. Courtesy the Library of Congress.

no longer exists, to 1826. Rothman makes the argument that Franklin and Armfield were working in the right place at the right time and that they were rewarded handsomely for their efforts. The business earned the men so much money that they were able to close shop after only a decade, retiring as wealthy men.

Less than thirty years later, with another owner in place at Franklin & Armfield, the Union army invaded Alexandria. While the owners escaped farther south with valuable humans in bondage in tow, the men in blue found a lone elderly man chained by himself in the backyard. His value was nil, so he was left behind. The story goes that the man was put into service by the Union army, perhaps performing tasks needed to repurpose the pens in the backyard as jail cells for captured Confederates.

Joseph McCoy Marker
Corner of Lee and Cameron Streets
Alexandria, VA 22314
www.alexandriava.gov/historic/blackhistory/default.aspx?id=114858

During the COVID pandemic, the City of Alexandria installed two new markers in Old Town, identifying the site of heinous crimes committed by

The Joseph McCoy Marker, installed in 2021.

white people: the lynchings of Black men. Lynching was a form of racial brutality and violence stemming from white supremacy, which permeated the era of Jim Crow for one hundred years between the end of Reconstruction and the start of the civil rights movement. Virginia documented more than one hundred lynchings between 1882 and 1968. In Alexandria, at least two lynchings were committed by white people against Black men: Joseph McCoy and Benjamin Thomas.

Lynching was used as a form of terror and control and often involved the tacit approval of local law enforcement. The first marker to be unveiled was the marker for Joseph McCoy. In 1897, McCoy was accused of raping a nine-year-old girl, the daughter of his employer. While he was jailed, a crowd descended on the building and dragged McCoy onto the street, where they hanged him, shot him several times, bludgeoned his skull and left him there for all to see. The purpose of such a public spectacle was to send a message to all Black Americans that justice and the law did not extend to them. A fair trial was nowhere to be found for McCoy, and no one was ever charged with his murder, even though hundreds of people witnessed and/or participated in the lynching. McCoy was buried in a pauper's grave.

Although the original lamppost where McCoy was hanged is no longer in place, the current post, with its new marker, serves to remind residents and visitors that American history, both local and national, has many such stories. The point of installing markers such as this one is to memorialize the dead, teach about inequality and racism and point to the importance of not only viewing the parts of history that are positive and pretty but also embracing, as much as is possible, all of our shared history, including its shortcomings, traumas and tragedies. And in the case of lynchings, especially, we need to remind the community that when people practice dehumanization—that is, removing the humanity of anyone who is unlike yourself—the result, as it has been for Black Americans over many centuries, is often despicable.

Under the auspices of the Alexandria Community Remembrance Project, following the precepts of the Equal Justice Initiative, the Joseph McCoy Marker was placed on April 23, 2021, almost 125 years after his lynching. The city drew people's attention to the memorial site by placing a wreath with McCoy's name on it in front of City Hall Plaza. Around the corner, another wreath at the new marker captured people's attention. Above the marker, attached to the pole, was a black-and-white flag that read, "A Man Was Lynched Today." This was a bold visual statement: this flag was originally created in the 1920s to bring awareness to the practice of lynching and to try to introduce legislation prohibiting violence against Black Americans. At the time, such laws were not passed, and Black people continued to live under fear and the ceaseless specter of violence.

The second lynching site, that of Benjamin Thomas's lynching, is on the southwest corner of Fairfax and King Streets. Thomas was sixteen years old in 1899, when he was hanged and shot—two hundred times. A part of his memorial marker reads:

> *On Monday, August 7, 1899, police had arrested Thomas on the word of an eight-year-old white neighbor and charged him with assaulting her.... white rioters attacked the City Jail on N. St. Asaph Street, where they seized and dragged Thomas for a half-mile on a cobblestone street, hitting him with bricks, iron, and stones as he cried out for his mother. Under the shadow of City Hall and the police station, he was stabbed, kicked, shot, and hanged....After the brutality inflicted on Thomas, his body was taken to Demaine Funeral Home on King Street. His mother, Elizabeth Thomas,*

"could not bear to look upon her boy."... The Black community mobilized to assist the Thomas family to raise funds to move his body from a pauper's grave into Douglass Cemetery, but the relocation was not recorded. There is still a question as to the final resting place of Benjamin Thomas.

Alexandria Black History Museum
Alexandria Library Sit-In
902 Wythe Street
Alexandria, VA 22314
www.alexandriava.gov/BlackHistory

Alexandria's Black History Museum is currently undergoing renovation and has not been open for the past two years, but plans are underway for a new exhibition on Moss H. Kendrix, a public relations icon in American culture, which is set to open in 2023.

The museum's founding is tied to the struggles and efforts of the twentieth-century civil rights movement. The City of Alexandria, like many municipalities in Virginia, found ways to fulfill federal legislation requiring "separate but equal" public facilities (for a most egregious example, examine the history of public education at the Robert Russa Moton Museum in Farmville). For public library access, Alexandria created a new library for Black residents in 1940. It was filled with secondhand books from the main Alexandria Library and donations. This first library was named after Robert H. Robinson, a formerly enslaved man who was the grandson of Caroline Branham, known to visitors of Mount Vernon as Martha Washington's personal enslaved maid. Alexandria finally integrated its library and school system around 1960, and a new purpose was given to the Robinson Library.

A Virginia Department of Historic Resources Marker tells the story:

On 21 August 1939, five young African American men applied for library cards at the new Alexandria Library to protest its whites-only policy. After being denied, William Evans, Edward Gaddis, Morris Murray, Clarence Strange, and Otto L. Tucker each selected a book from the shelves, sat down, and read quietly. The men were arrested and charged with disorderly conduct, despite their polite demeanor. Local attorney Samuel W. Tucker, who helped plan the protest, represented them in court. The judge never issued a ruling. In 1940, Alexandria opened the Robert Robinson Library for African Americans. Desegregation of the library system began by 1959.

The Alexandria Library Sit-In Department of Historic Resources Marker, located close to the intersection of North Washington and Queen Streets.

The Alexandria Society for the Preservation of Black Heritage, along with alumni from Parker-Gray High School, a school in one of the city's historic neighborhoods, came together to transform the library into a history and research museum. A new book about this groundbreaking part of Alexandrian history is coming in 2022—see Brenda Mitchell Powell's

Public in Name Only: The 1939 Alexandria Library Sit-In Demonstration (Amherst: University of Massachusetts Press).

Today, after successive waves of redevelopment, the museum features curated exhibits on Black history in Alexandria, spaces for lectures and a museum store filled with books that will enhance your own education. Contemporary works of art also depict themes important to Black history, and the museum continues to evolve by creating virtual exhibits, such as "Preserving Their Names," a collecting initiative centered on the public death of George Floyd in 2020. Historic Alexandria continues to digitize collections across all its museums, including the Black History Museum. The link to begin your own search for interesting objects is historicalexandria.pastperfectonline.com.

Alexandria African American Hall of Fame
Charles Houston Recreation Center
901 Wythe Street
Alexandria, VA 22314
www.alexandriaafricanamericanhalloffame.org

The most recent addition to the Alexandria African American Hall of Fame is the bronze statue of basketball hero Earl Francis Lloyd. An all-American athlete, Lloyd became the first Black basketball player in the NBA, playing for the Washington Capitols. As an Alexandrian, Lloyd attended Parker-Gray, the segregated high school, and was later drafted by West Virginia College (later West Virginia State University). After playing in more than five hundred NBA games, he became a coach for the Pistons in Detroit, the first Black coach in NBA history. Between breaking the color barrier in basketball, Lloyd was drafted by the United States Army and served in Korea.

Lloyd appears in seven different halls of fame, and an earlier bronze statue of him is included in the National Basketball Hall of Fame, as well as at his alma mater. A group of his devoted and grateful colleagues raised $50,000 to create this newest version of Lloyd's monument, showing the six-foot-five-inch-tall player dribbling the ball down the court, eyes forward, hand gripping the ball. Alexandria's desire to celebrate and commemorate the legacy of Lloyd will go a step further when the 1000 block of Montgomery Street is renamed in his honor.

The Earl Lloyd statue at the Charles Houston Recreation Center.

Contrabands and Freedmen Cemetery Memorial
1001 South Washington Street
Alexandria, VA 22314
www.alexandriava.gov/FreedmenMemorial

In 2021, Alexandria's Contrabands and Freedmen Cemetery Memorial became one of the newest sites on the African American Civil Right Network. The National Park Service manages this network of historic sites across the country; it connects fifty-seven special places that tell the stories of the civil rights movement and the continuing struggle for equality through equity. This memorial is a unique testament to the ways in which racism has played out in Alexandria. This story of the cemetery is this: this area was the burial ground for 1,800 Black Americans in the 1860s; 600 graves have been identified today. The U.S. Army established the cemetery for contrabands and freedmen at the end of the Civil War, indicating the high number of Black Americans who came to Alexandria to escape bondage and to restart their lives by working to support the U.S. Army, which had control of the city throughout the war. Unfortunately, the influx of people was so great and

Stones laid out in the shape of coffin—both adult- and child-sized—at the Contrabands and Freedmen Cemetery Memorial.

the living conditions in Alexandria were so poor that many people died from disease. The last burial occurred in 1869.

The cemetery fell into disrepair and then abuse, when, in the mid-twentieth century, a gas station and an office building were erected on the site. The Friends of the Freedmen Cemetery formed to help the City of Alexandria and the National Park Service regain knowledge of the cemetery and make plans for memorializing it after finding the locations of the graves with ground-penetrating radar. Finally, in 2014, organizers who raised funds together dedicated a new public art installation, comprising stone walls and a large bronze monument. Alexandrian architect C.J. Howard provided the overall design concept, which did not disturb any of the graves.

Contrabands and Freedmen Cemetery Memorial is the first site in Virginia to be added to the African American Civil Rights Network, and it is the oldest site in the network. This designation heightens the importance of the historic site, which is already listed in the National Register of Historic Places, the Virginia Landmarks Register and the National Underground Railroad Network to Freedom. Visit the African American Civil Rights Network here: www.nps.gov/subjects/civilrights/african-american-civil-rights-network.

African American Heritage Memorial Park
500 Holland Lane
Alexandria, VA 22314
www.alexandriava.gov/historic/blackhistory/default.aspx?id=37348

All is not what it seems in this complicated landscape of Alexandria. Part of an urban redevelopment project—over-scaled residential and commercial buildings comprise this corner of the city—the area is historic and, as it turns out, the burial place for at least twenty people, a rediscovery that prevented the open space from further development. Instead, developers donated the green space with water running through it to the City of Alexandria, which redeveloped the area into African American Heritage Park and a small wetland naturalist reserve. So, when you walk through this park, you might come into contact with waterfowl, such as ducks or herons, birds common to Alexandria, but you will also walk (or run) directly past remaining grave markers that have stood the test of time—and neglect.

As you might have guessed from the introductory words above, this is a small park that packs in a lot. The central feature of Black commemoration

Gravestones at the African American Heritage Memorial Park in the Carlyle section of Alexandria.

is a bronzed installation of three tree-like pillars standing in a low-ringed configuration, with an artistic and documentary text on a raised mound, which represents a burial. Called *Truths that Rise from the Roots—Remembered*, the piece's artist, Jerome Meadows, designed these bronze trees to stand twelve to fifteen feet tall, overlooking the landscape that was once home to the Black Baptist Cemetery. On the trees and mounds are historic photographic images etched into the metal surface, with names and information, as well as symbols important to Black culture, some of which are African in origin, accompanying them.

Farther along the trail in the park, visitors walk or run alongside the creek/river and can read about the small but significant wetland that supports flora and fauna. Looking up and over the park, rows and rows of gleaming white headstones alert you to another special cemetery: the Alexandria National Cemetery, which, in addition to the many thousands of burial sites of white soldiers, also includes the graves of buffalo soldiers.

Douglass Cemetery
1367–1473 Wilkes Street
Alexandria, VA 22314

Named for famed abolitionist and Black leader Frederick Douglass—a man who self-emancipated by escaping the plantation where he was born into slavery—this cemetery is getting renewed attention, thanks, in part, to climate change and, in part, to Virginia's recognition that it has not done enough to preserve and share Black history. Located in a marshy area that historically had a stream running through it, the cemetery was abandoned at some point, hastening its deterioration. Many gravesites have no grave markers, and the stones that are there have been pushed up and are falling over due to the shifting earth underneath. In addition, a new apartment building, constructed at the edge of the historic cemetery, contributes to the sense of disunion felt at the site—bright new walls standing in contrast to rows of historic stones standing in waves in the marshy soil, ready to topple over. The cemetery dates to 1827. There are about 600 headstones in view, but there are closer to 1,900 burial sites.

Douglass Cemetery can be found in a section of the city where multiple cemeteries are located, joined at the seams but managed by different churches. In addition to Douglass Cemetery, you can walk along to see burial sites at Trinity United Methodist Church and Christ Church Episcopal Cemetery,

Right: The Douglass Cemetery
sign.

Below: Standing gravestones at
Douglass Cemetery indicating
changing soil due to water erosion
and a lack of maintenance
over time, as the cemetery
was abandoned. The City of
Alexandria and others are
working to address the situation.

A view of headstones in Alexandria National Cemetery.

some dating to 1808 (once the churchyard was filled, this second site for burials was utilized). The cemeteries are marked with multiple obelisks, and in the distance, you can see the Washington Masonic Memorial, another structure pointing toward the heavens. At the end of a cul-de-sac is the largest cemetery in this area, Alexandria National Cemetery, a military cemetery that predates Arlington but is also filled with rows of recognizable white marble headstones. Also inside Alexandria National Cemetery is a memorial to four men who lost their lives chasing John Wilkes Booth after he assassinated Lincoln, as well as the grave markers for five Black soldiers, then called buffalo soldiers.

7

SOME NEIGHBORHOOD HISTORY

DEL RAY, SEMINARY HILL AND ROSEMONT

Centered on Mount Vernon Avenue, Del Ray is a neighborhood in the city of Alexandria with a sense of place all its own. Beloved by its community members for its feel of family friendliness, Del Ray is also considered the artsy side of town, a great place to get a great meal (and drinks). It's also known for its Wellness District that supports holistic health businesses—more than forty, in fact. Del Ray is busy throughout the year, hosting special events such as the Holiday Market, which has been running for twenty-five years; Art on the Avenue, which is held on the first Saturday in October; and a Taste of Del Ray, which is held in June. Bikers, walkers and runners make use of Del Ray's charming flat streets, and visitors take advantage of its proximity to Old Town. Colorful murals are very much a part of Del Ray; they advertise businesses within the neighborhood and promote community pride, love and, sometimes, politics. Like much of Alexandria, Del Ray is an expensive area of the city to live in. Attesting to the neighborhood's strong, separate identification, the area has its own business association (economic development). See visitdelray.com, whose tagline is: "Where Main Street Still Exists." Some of the public art and public history in Del Ray include the following.

Captain "Rocky" Versace Plaza
Alexandria Vietnam Veterans Memorial
Mount Vernon Recreation Center
2701 Commonwealth Avenue
Alexandria, VA 22305
www.alexandriava.gov/recreation/default.aspx?id=120948

This is a bronze sculptural group dedicated to U.S. Army captain Humbert Roque "Rocky" Versace, the son of an American soldier and a West Point graduate who died in Vietnam. Sixty-eight Alexandrians perished in the Vietnam War, including marines, infantrymen, airmen and sailors, but Versace was the only person from Alexandria to be awarded a Medal of Honor from the Vietnam War era. In 2002, members of the 1959 class of the United States Military Academy at West Point banded together, along with their family and friends, to create the memorial, which is both the bronze sculpture and the plaza that contains the names of the city's sixty-seven Vietnam veterans (in addition to Versace)—men and women, both those killed in action and missing in action. The story of Captain Versace is an anguished one. He was in a prisoner of war (POW) camp with leg wounds for almost two years before he was killed. Versace was close to ending his tour of duty and enrolling in a Catholic seminary when he was killed. The location of his remains is unknown, but Versace has a memorial cenotaph in Arlington National Cemetery.

Antonio Tobias "Toby" Mendez sculpted the figure of the soldier playing with Vietnamese children. Around the figure is a circular bench with the names of the other Alexandrians killed in action, the inscriptions following a chronology of death from the first in 1963 to the last a decade later. Inside the recreation center is a display case with information about Versace and the Vietnam War era. Around the building, you can find a large outdoor mural of Del Ray and its residents.

The Birchmere
3701 Mount Vernon Avenue
Alexandria, VA 22305
www.birchmere.com

The Birchmere is a music hall–style venue that was opened in 1966 (so, yes, it passes the fifty-year-old mark, a traditional age for a place to be called "historic"). Inside are walls filled with signed posters from past musical acts

Right: Captain "Rocky" Versace and the Alexandria Vietnam Veterans Memorial in the Del Ray section of Alexandria.

Below: The mural façade of the Birchmere.

and a gift shop, where performers can sell their merchandise after shows. The center of the building is a dark, five-hundred-seat space with a low stage. The views from most seats make one feel like they are not too far from the performers, and the sound quality is easy on the ears. The venue opens early for patrons who come to eat and drink, and plates are cleared away in time for the show to begin. The Birchmere is retro without intending to be. There is nothing pretentious about the place, and it's a great antidote to all that is so bright, shiny and new in Alexandria and South Fairfax County. It's a place for music lovers who don't need light and sound shows—just the music of their favorite singers and bands. In 2021, Wynonna Judd, a Prince and Fleetwood Mac tribute band and Steve Earle and the Dukes were all scheduled to perform. In between, comedy nights and other events round out the venue's offerings. It's a great place to see your favorites, old and new, and it's a treasure from an earlier musical era.

Dogs of Del Ray Mural
Stomping Ground (Facing Pat Miller Neighborhood Square)
2309 Mount Vernon Avenue
Alexandria, VA 22301

Artist Patrick Kirwin was commissioned to create a new mural for Del Ray, this one dedicated to the pups of the neighborhood, all in the name of fundraising. Two citizens, Karen Johnson and Pat Miller, came up with the idea, which, in the end, raised $4,500 for the Animal Welfare League of Alexandria. The mural is a colorful, loving tribute to man's best friend, but it is also an indicator of the city's dedication to volunteerism,

The *Dogs of Del Ray* mural by Patrick Kirwin.

civic engagement and community development. Getting together and committing to a community project is a common theme in Alexandria, and in this case, PawsGo, the organization run by Johnson, hit gold. Del Ray, like much of Alexandria, is a dog-centric area, and in the end, more than two hundred dogs were put on a waiting list to be painted. Although this is the only dog-centric spot highlighted in the book, it is easy to see that Alexandria is welcoming to dogs—water bowls appear on sidewalks, and restaurant patios are open to them, too. Specific businesses, such as the Barkhaus, exist just for them and their owners. Cats are also not forgotten (see Mount Purrnon for evidence).

SEMINARY HILL

Outside of Old Town and Del Ray, residential neighborhoods with small-scale industrial buildings and commercial strips have become the norm. The Seminary Hill neighborhood is urban and dense, making these historic spots important for their open, green spaces and the historic stories they tell.

Virginia Theological Seminary
3737 Seminary Road
Alexandria, VA 22304
www.vts.edu

Virginia Theological Seminary made the *New York Times* in 2021 due to the religious school's decision to pay reparations to the descendants of the enslaved workers who built and labored at the school between its founding in 1823 through the Civil War and after. Although the seminary announced such plans in 2019, the following years saw a rise in awareness of social justice initiatives around the country. The seminary was originally supported by enslavers and those who supported slavery, most infamously Francis Scott Key, who wrote the "Star-Spangled Banner" and who was an active prosecutor of abolitionist journalists. To read the historic marker located at the site today is to lose all sense of this essential part of its history (this is a historical marker that needs rewriting). The contemporary leadership of the seminary recognized that even after the Civil War ended, Black Americans worked at the school without adequate pay and poor

Seminary Hill's ruined chapel as a memorial and the *Mary as Prophet* sculpture by Margaret Adams Parker.

treatment, especially during the years of Jim Crow laws. The seminary has begun its reparations work by creating a $1.7 million fund, which it began dispersing to the descendants of families in February 2021. The fund will continue to grow, allowing for annual checks of $2,100 to family members identified by genealogists.

Today, on the seminary's campus, which is open for visitors, there exists Victorian-era buildings, such as Aspinwall Hall from 1858, mixed with modern structures. An unusual and beautiful memorial, a garden with benches for quiet contemplation, was created from an abandoned and ruined chapel. Inside the buildings, modern stained glass can be viewed, while outside, near the memorial chapel garden, is the statue of *Mary as Prophet* by Margaret Adams Parker (2015). Visitors are welcome to walk the historic campus.

Fort Ward Museum and Historic Site
4301 West Braddock Road
Alexandria, VA 22304
www.alexandria.gov/FortWard

This small city park is filled with layers of history that are central to Alexandrian and American history. The area was built up as one of the many defenses of Washington, D.C., during the Civil War. Fort Ward was the fifth-largest fort in the ring of defenses around the capital city (a total of 164). Today, visitors can tour the reconstructed five-bastion redoubt. At the historic fort, there is a ceremonial gate through which visitors walk the earthen works and strategically placed cannons that were used to help the Union army guard both Alexandria—an essential transportation center—and the capital. Only one bastion has been reconstructed, providing a sense of the size and scale of the fort during the war. Earthen fortifications were constructed from the area's dirt, which was readily available, free and strong enough when built up and shaped into ramparts (walls) above

Earthworks and cannons at the Fort Ward Historic Site, part of the defenses of Washington, D.C., during the Civil War.

parapets (slopes) to provide a protective layer against assault from mortars and projectiles. Dirt, in this case, was better than stone. A dry trench called a moat surrounded forts; downed trees used for fencing provided an extra layer of protection.

Major General John G. Barnard, a West Point graduate, oversaw the construction of the Civil War defenses for Washington, D.C. Fort Ward was named after the first Union army officer to be killed during the war, Commander James H. Ward, and was considered a feat of nineteenth-century military engineering. According to the National Park Service, Washington, D.C.—surrounded by states sympathetic to the Confederate cause—became one of the most heavily fortified cities in the world. Outside of the fort proper is a re-created officer's hut and a museum that contains exhibits and a research library. The museum just reopened after a closure for renovations. It has a colorful collection of Zouave uniforms and information about the death of Colonel Ellsworth at the beginning of the war. Zouaves, first appearing as light infantry for the French army in the early nineteenth century, fought on both sides of the Civil War.

After the Civil War, a Black community grew here from the descendants of the refugees and contrabands who escaped enslavement and the Deep South. But over time, the park reemerged as a place to remember the Civil War. This happened one hundred years after the war, during the tumultuous era of the civil rights movement in the 1960s. The City of Alexandria gained ownership of the grounds, moving Black families out of the fort and its grounds, and rededicated the park to Civil War memory, thereby neglecting and marginalizing the long history of Black Americans whose lives were tightly bound together here in a mutually supportive community. The graves of many of the residents of the fort's community still lie under the earth at Fort Ward.

In 2021, the City of Alexandria engaged with a public history process, whereby the community gathered and determined how best to protect, mark and interpret the Black burial areas at Fort Ward. There are four major burial areas within the grounds of Fort Ward, including the Old Graveyard, established in 1897; the Adams family burial site, which includes the grave of community matriarch Clara Adams; the Clark family burial site; and the Jackson Cemetery, which was established on land that was purchased by fort resident James Jackson in 1884 and that was once part of the earlier Civil War Union fort. This work, led by the Office of Historic Alexandria and community members, is part of a broad movement across Virginia to address the dire neglect suffered by many Black cemeteries, including

The interior view of the officer's hut re-created on the grounds of the Fort Ward Museum and Historic Site.

those at Shockoe Bottom in Richmond and as seen, most egregiously, in the discovery of headstones that had been dumped into the Potomac River from the Columbian Harmony Cemetery in Washington, D.C. Virginia state senator Richard Stuart discovered that the headstones from the Black cemetery were used as erosion control for his riverfront farm; they had been dumped there during a commercial construction project. The 2022 Virginia General Assembly budget provided $25 million in funding to address several social justice projects across the state, including $5 million to transform that cemetery into a memorial.

Today, Fort Ward is used by area residents of Seminary Hill for walking, while students of the Civil War visit to find information on military history. Black Americans remember Fort Ward for its role in the lives of other Black Americans over the course of more than one hundred years. Visit Fort Ward for all these reasons.

ROSEMONT

Located between Del Ray and Seminary Hill, Rosemont is a sliver of a neighborhood in Alexandria, but it is historic, as it was the first planned neighborhood expansion out of Old Town. Rosemont became a National Historic District in recognition of its historic architecture and beginnings as a "streetcar" suburb for commuters to Washington, D.C. This is an area popular with cyclists, due to its many hills, which get the heart pumping.

Ivy Hill Cemetery
2823 King Street
Alexandria, VA 22302
www.ivyhill.org/societyindex

One of the quieter historic spaces in Alexandria, Ivy Hill Cemetery has been in existence since 1837, when it was the Smith family cemetery. The cemetery's growth by the middle of the nineteenth century prompted its incorporation in 1856. The twenty-two-acre cemetery and green space is a perfect place to take a walk and travel through time while also experiencing

Firemen's Monument at the Ivy Hill Cemetery in Rosemont.

the Piedmont's flora and fauna. The winding road through the cemetery is a microcosm of the Piedmont itself, with rolling green hills and a variety of trees. Not surprisingly, the cemetery is a draw for birdwatchers. Ivy Hill contains Alexandria's firemen's monument; a memorial to 9/11; the Green family, known for their furniture-making company; and the Stabler-Leadbeater family, who owned the apothecary of the same name in Old Town. One of the most interesting burial sites in Ivy Hill is that of Wernher von Braun (1912–1977), a German scientist and Nazi turned NASA employee. Visitors leave small mementos at the site, including German and NASA flags and tiny toy rocket ships.

8

HISTORY ALONG THE GEORGE WASHINGTON MEMORIAL PARKWAY

S outh Fairfax County combines urban areas and shopping centers, national parks, historic sites and museums, waterfront sites and recreational areas, including spaces for golfing, biking and kayaking, among other offerings. Within Fairfax County are the independent cities of Arlington, Alexandria and Fairfax, and they are surrounded by county towns. George Washington's Mount Vernon, one of the most visited and well known (and first) historic house museums in the United States, is located here. As is the home of another founding father, George Mason, who wrote the Virginia Declaration of Rights, a document that shaped the way Thomas Jefferson crafted the Declaration of Independence for the United States of America.

In addition to the city of Alexandria, a large part of South Fairfax County is called Alexandria as well. This area, "Below the Beltway," has several Alexandria zip codes and is bounded by Highway 495 to the north and I-95 to the west. The following section of this book, comprising the two last chapters, will travel this area of South Fairfax County, encompassing some special historic places in Alexandria and some beyond in Mason Neck and Lorton. The rest of Fairfax County is also packed with things to do and historical places to visit, but that's for another book. For information regarding the rest of Fairfax County, please visit the Fairfax County Visitor Center at the Tysons Corner Center in Tyson, Virginia, or visit online at www.FXVA.com.

George Washington Memorial Parkway
Maryland, District of Columbia, Virginia
www.nps.gov/gwmp/index

A dedicatory bronze plaque that is used to mark the inception of the "Mount Vernon Memorial Highway," later called the George Washington Memorial Parkway, circa 1932.

When the United States reached the two hundredth birthday of George Washington, it decided to build him a parkway. What could be more American than that? The Department of the Interior is the behemoth federal organization that manages more than 450 million acres of land on behalf of the American people, including national forests such as the George Washington and Jefferson National Forests in the Appalachian Mountains of Virginia. Within the Department of the Interior is the National Park Service, a large preservation organization that focuses on maintaining parks, monuments, historic houses and, yes, parkways (think Blue Ridge Parkway). The creation of the George Washington Memorial Parkway was meant to offer a twenty-five-mile-long scenic route from Washington, D.C., through Alexandria (Washington's urban home) to Mount Vernon, Washington's rural home and plantation. The timing was not coincidental; in 1932, Americans were celebrating the bicentennial of George Washington's birthday, and the automobile was becoming ever more affordable. This corresponded with a decade of intense interest in American history, as many cities and states were celebrating milestone anniversaries and preservation was heating up in places like Colonial Williamsburg.

The George Washington Memorial Parkway was authorized by an act of Congress, and at the time, it was called "America's most modern motorway." The parkway is an example of a "living memorial," that is, a place that actively serves the public and therefore "lives" in a way that a static stone or bronze monument does not. Other examples of living memorials include libraries, swimming pools, parks and schools.

There are historic sites, memorials, recreational areas, nature viewing areas and more along the entirety of the parkway. In Arlington County, for example, you can visit the U.S. Marine Corps War Memorial, Netherlands

Carillon, Women in Military Service for America Memorial, Arlington House/Robert E. Lee Memorial, Arlington National Cemetery, L.B.J. Memorial Grove/Columbia Island Marina, Theodore Roosevelt Island, Air Force Memorial and Navy and Merchant Marine Memorial. Expanded northward in the 1950s and 1960s, the George Washington Memorial Parkway has a separate section called the Clara Barton Highway that travels from the Chain Bridge in Washington, D.C., and north into Maryland. Farther north along the parkway, you can visit Great Falls Park, Clara Barton National Historic Site, Glen Echo Park, Turkey Run Park, Claude Moore Colonial Farm and Fort Marcy. The parkway and its pedestrian twin, the Mount Vernon Trail, which intersects with the Potomac Heritage National Scenic Trail, a network of trails extending from the Upper Ohio River Basin to the Chesapeake Bay, are filled with connections to many trail systems, including the Appalachian Trail.

For this book, we are concerned with the southern section of the George Washington Memorial Parkway in Alexandria and South Fairfax County. The parkway connects Old Town Alexandria to Mount Vernon via a paved and busy parkway—meaning curving roads, vistas across the Potomac River and swaths of green, treed landscapes. Bronze plaques to George Washington can be spotted with frequency along the parkway, as can single clumps of memorial trees that were usually, again, planted for Washington. One of the most popular pieces of the parkway is its Mount Vernon Trail. Running alongside the paved roadway but often veering off to follow the natural curves where land meets the river, the Mount Vernon Trail is a popular walking/biking recreational trail. It is also used by commuters to get into Washington, D.C. If you are visiting, there are bike shops in the city of Alexandria that can supply you with a rental.

Mount Vernon Trail
www.mountvernontrail.org

This paved multiuse trail runs for twenty miles between the city of Alexandria and George Washington's Mount Vernon, encompassing more than nine hundred acres of protected green space. As a linear park that buffers both sides of the George Washington Memorial Parkway, there are multiple smaller parks within its borders, as well as historic sites and nature areas. The Mount Vernon Trail is also part of the East Coast Greenway, a bike trail that runs from Maine to Florida (www.greenway.org).

Belle Haven Park
George Washington Memorial Parkway
Alexandria, VA 22307

This large parking area with picnic tables and open green space near Dyke Marsh Wildlife Preserve doesn't much resemble the earliest White colonial settlement on the banks of the Potomac River. But a descriptive Virginia Department of Historic Resources marker titled "Colonial Fort" provides an interpretation to help visitors reimagine this low-lying stretch of marshy land. The marker reads:

> *Nearby, at John Mathews's land on Hunting Creek, Governor William Berkeley constructed a fort authorized by the Virginia House of Burgesses on 21 Sept. 1674. Militiamen from Lancaster, Middlesex, and Northumberland Counties garrisoned the fort under command of Capt. Peter Knight. The fort defended the northern frontier of the colony against the Susquehannocks and other Indian groups. Berkeley planned for it and other forts to serve as buffers and thereby enable the English and the Indians to coexist peacefully. Some colonists, especially those led by Nathaniel Bacon, favored a more aggressive approach. As a result, Bacon's Rebellion erupted in 1675–76.*

Dyke Marsh Wildlife Preserve
George Washington Memorial Parkway
Alexandria, VA 22307
www.fodm.org

Dyke Marsh is a special place on the George Washington Memorial Parkway; it is the last remnant of an extensive freshwater tidal marsh, the kind which was known up and down the Potomac River until infill began to change the areas where the land and water met, creating new space for building projects, such as roads and parkways. Dredging from the 1940s to the 1970s removed more than half of the original marsh, and today, climate change is accelerating its erosion. Tidal marshes are critical habitats for many species of wildfowl, birds, insects and natural flora. Today, Dyke Marsh is a birder's paradise because of the number of species that can be seen there, including great blue herons and green night herons. Visitors can park at Belle Haven and walk Dyke Marsh, and for those with kayaks or canoes, you can paddle your way in. Although it is managed by the National Park Service as part of the George Washington Memorial Parkway, the Friends of Dyke Marsh, a not-for-profit organization, helps program the nature site by hosting a bird walk every Sunday morning at 8:00 a.m. The group meets at the south parking lot at Belle Haven. It is also active in removing invasive species, including English ivy, kudzu and more. Some of the insects and animals seen at Dyke Marsh include the ruby meadowhawk dragonfly, skipper butterfly, eastern painted turtle and, new in 2021, buff-breasted sandpipers and pink roseate spoonbills.

Fort Hunt Park
George Washington Memorial Parkway
8999 Fort Hunt Road
Alexandria, VA 22308
www.nps.gov/gwmp/planyourvisit/forthunt

Fort Hunt Park is an open space for passive recreation, such as walking, picnicking, dog walking, bird watching and biking. It is also a historic site situated amid a residential section of South Fairfax County, and it is connected to the George Washington Memorial Parkway and the Mount Vernon Trail. Just five miles south of Washington, D.C., Fort Hunt was a fort from the Spanish-American War that never saw action, the site of two active Civilian Conservation Corps (CCC) camps and a site for military intelligence work during World War I and II. The remains of some of this militarization can be found in several spots of the park today, including a series of concrete bunkers and artillery platforms. A wooden clapboard house stands sentinel at the entrance, empty and likely dating from the first decade of the twentieth century. The National Park Service added only the most basic amenities to Fort Hunt Park, such as a bathroom, but the park is popular for its free parking, open green space and the fact that a circular, paved road encompasses the park and is used by walkers, dog walkers, bikers and more. Also located within the boundaries of the park is the Commonwealth of Virginia's Horse Police Unit.

One of the more unique memorials in Alexandria and South Fairfax County is the King George VI Witness Tree. Although this fact is sometimes forgotten today, trees have been used as memorials for time immemorial; Fort Hunt Park is home to one of the more unusual examples of this. The Witness Tree was planted in 1939 to commemorate King George VI's visit

Concrete gun mounts at the Fort Hunt Park.

to the United States. George was the first reigning monarch to visit North America, and he did so to garner support for the British cause during a troubling time in Europe: the rise of the Nazism. King George and his wife, Queen Elizabeth, were on their way to Canada, a commonwealth country, but after receiving an invitation from President Franklin Delano Roosevelt, they made an excursion to Washington, D.C. On their way from the White House to Mount Vernon, where the king laid a wreath at Washington's tomb, the party stopped at Fort Hunt to visit the CCC camp.

The purpose of CCC camps was not unlike the purpose of the Works Progress Administration (WPA), both national programs under Franklin's New Deal. The CCC was created to provide employment during the country's Great Depression and to undertake restoration and infrastructure projects on behalf of the country. At Fort Hunt, the CCC did restoration work. To remember this remarkable visit from the reigning monarch, a friend of the king named Sir Richard St. Barbe Baker arranged for two pin oak trees to be planted there. Only one survives today, standing by itself between the huge chain link fence that surrounds the park and the concrete drive that serves runners, walkers and bikers so well. Baker was a tree man, an active biologist and botanist, and his choice of oak was predicated on the environment of Fort Hunt Park. Today, as the environment receives ever more attention due to climate change, oak trees are again in the news. A recent article in the *New York Times* encouraged people to plant oaks due to the amount of life they support—from birds and bears to caterpillars and spiders.

What came after the English monarchy's visit to Fort Hunt was, of course, World War II. Although you wouldn't guess it today from what is visibly left of the park's landscape, Fort Hunt was the primary military facility for intelligence work, coordinating interrogations and escape and invasion activities, during the war. A separate, upright, standing stone memorial remembers this aspect of Fort Hunt history—look for the flagpole with the wording for "P.O. Box 1142," which reads:

> *This flagpole is dedicated to the veterans of P.O. Box 1142, who served this country as members of two military intelligence service (MIS) programs during WWII. Their top-secret work here at Fort Hunt not only contributed to the Allied victory but also led to strategic advances in military intelligence and scientific technology that directly influenced the Cold War and the Space Race. The MIS-X program communicated with American military personnel held captive by the enemy Axis forces and attempted to coordinate their escape. The larger MIS-Y program carried out the interrogation of nearly 4,000 enemy prisoners of war and scientists who were processed at this camp.*

Today, Fort Hunt Park is surrounded by the Fort Hunt neighborhood, a mix of mid-twentieth century homes and much larger twenty-first-century mansions. Some houses have bronze plaques that read, "This home rests upon the five farms of Mount Vernon, estate of President George Washington, registered by the Neighborhood Friends of Historic Mount Vernon."

River Farm
7931 East Boulevard Drive
Alexandria, VA 22308
www.ahsgardening.org/about-river-farm

River Farm, one of the five farms owned by George Washington and thus part of his original eight thousand acres, today consists of twenty-five acres of publicly accessible space. Beloved by neighbors and visitors for its gardens, a meadow down to the Potomac River and historic buildings, River Farm was in the news a great deal in 2020–21. The owners of the property, the American Horticultural Society, put the entire property on the market in November 2020 for $32.9 million. Neighbors, activists, city and county leaders and more jumped into action to stave off the potential turnover of the naturalistic property to private developer hands. After a year of negotiations, board resignations and public activism, River Farm was taken off the market and returned to use as the headquarters of the society, with renewed plans for more preservation and public accessibility.

Like much of Virginia and the United States, material evidence of land use and settlement exists in the archaeological record. At River Farm, Indigenous peoples actively used the site for centuries before Giles Brent, an English colonizer, purchased the land in the 1650s. A century later, George Washington became the property's next owner, and it remained in the Washington family until 1859, when the Mount Vernon Ladies' Association acquired Mount Vernon and began making plans to restore it for the public. The American Horticultural Society was brought to task by groups like Save

The exterior view of the River Farm on the Potomac River, one of George Washington's original five farms.

River Farm and many other individuals and politicians, because $1 million had been given to the society by philanthropist Enid A. Haupt. The basic premise of philanthropy is that there is a contract between a donor and an organization: the organization agrees to use the donation for only the identified purpose, and to go around or negate that agreement is unethical.

This was not your average house listing on Zillow (if you purchased River Farm today, your property taxes would be almost $200,000 per year). The listing from Compass Real Estate read:

> *HOME AMENITIES: Over 4,000 square feet of entertaining space; large, covered porch and smaller enclosed porch; original trim, windows and floors; six bedrooms, six bathrooms; spacious slate patio; extensive formal and informal gardens with historic plantings; carriage house; cottage.*

> *HISTORY: River Farm's first owners were the Brents, an English Catholic family active in early colonial Maryland. In 1653 or 1654, Giles Brent obtained 1,800 acres for his son, Giles Jr. and his wife, a princess of the Piscataway tribe. This grant of 1,800 acres, named Piscataway Neck, included the land that is now River Farm. In 1760, George Washington bought the land for £1,210. Along with the purchase of three other nearby tracts, Washington consolidated his holdings into a single, contiguous plantation of approximately 7,400 acres. River Farm became the northernmost of Washington's five farms. Malcolm Matheson bought the property in 1919 and remodeled the home into a charming early-20th-century country estate that stands today. In 1973, American Horticultural Society (AHS) board member and philanthropist Enid Annenberg Haupt provided funds for the AHS to purchase the property. The grounds now house the offices of AHS and are used for weddings, events and gardening.*

In the compressed open space availability of South Fairfax County—and after the COVID-19 pandemic, which saw Americans embrace and actively use green spaces more than ever before—the potential sale of River Farm to a private buyer or developer who would likely turn the property into a new subdivision was thought to not be in the spirit of the original donor's intention when she gave $1 million in the 1970s for the property's purchase. A proposal by Northern Virginia Parks Authority and the Northern Virginia Conservation Trust to purchase the property for $16 million in the spring of 2021 was not accepted, but the organization recognized its role as the legal caretaker of the original donation for green space for the public. A house next door called River View was on the market at the same time for $60 million, indicative of both the desirability of the Potomac River views and the bloated housing market of the United States during the pandemic.

George Washington's Mount Vernon
3200 Mount Vernon Memorial Highway
Mount Vernon, VA 22121
www.mountvernon.org

In 1846, a group of women banded together to form the Mount Vernon Ladies' Association (the MVLA). Their aim was to save a dilapidated plantation house on a hillside overlooking the Potomac River. This house, with its broad porch roof propped up with ship masts, belonged to a man who was remembered as "first in war, first in peace, and first in the hearts of his countrymen." The man remembered was, of course, George Washington, and this house was once the center of an eight-thousand-acre plantation along the Potomac River, comprising five separate farms labored on by 317 enslaved men, women and children. The MVLA undertook its work as a leader in the preservation movement at a time when women were mostly seen and not heard—before women had the right to vote, before colleges accepted women as equally as men, before the Civil War and emancipation. Mount Vernon, in other words, has been a witness to momentous change.

Originally called Little Hunting Creek Plantation, named for a tributary of the Potomac River that traveled through Alexandria and South Fairfax County, the house and surrounding plantation were owned by Lawrence Washington, Washington's older half brother and stand-in father figure. Lawrence named the place Mount Vernon after Admiral Vernon, whom he had served under in the British navy. George got his hands on the house and property—and this included human beings—when his brother died, and his sister-in-law sold the property and the people to him. Today, a portrait of Lawrence hangs in Washington's study, where he sits on the wall as a reminder of the earlier life of Mount Vernon, when the house was not yet a mansion.

George Washington is quoted as saying, "I would rather be on my farm than emperor of the world," and it is this place that drew him away from accepting a life term as president of the new United States. He did serve

Some of the people (and animals) who interpret George Washington's Mount Vernon for hundreds of thousands of visitors every year.

two terms as president, setting the example for all others to follow until today (excluding, of course, Franklin Delano Roosevelt during World War II), but it was often Mount Vernon that occupied his thoughts and desires. Washington expanded the house by adding two massive wings on its north and south sides, a colonnaded porch for viewing the Potomac River and a cupola. A large Palladian glass window in the two-story "New Room" showcased the gilded frames of his personal painting collection within. What exactly did Washington collect, you ask? Paintings of riverways, of course. The final touch on the house was a weathervane of a dove of peace on the cupola—placed there after the end of the Revolution.

After Washington's death in 1799 and that of his wife, Martha, soon after, Mount Vernon began to deteriorate. But people visited anyway, as this is where the Washingtons were buried. In his book *The Property of the Nation, George Washington's Tomb, Mount Vernon, and the Memory of the First President* (Lawrence: University Press of Kansas, 2019), Matthew R. Costello tracks the decades of work to preserve Washington's memory. Many wanted Washington's remains to be moved to a new memorial in the District of Columbia. In the meantime, people came from all over to visit Mount Vernon because the gravesite was there—the house was of less interest and continued to fall ever deeper into neglect. That is, until the members of the Mount Vernon Ladies' Association banded together to purchase the home and some of the remaining land from the Washington family.

With time and money, Mount Vernon became an iconic historical site for Virginia, drawing in hundreds of thousands of visitors per year due to its proximity to Washington, D.C. (the official flag of the District of Columbia has three stars and two bars referencing the Washington family crest). Although the property was reduced in size over two centuries by Washington himself and then by subsequent developers to make way for housing and other uses, the core plantation, the Mansion House Farm, has been re-created to include outbuildings for agricultural endeavors, as well as four period gardens, animal pens, a greenhouse, a bunkhouse for the enslaved community and a wheat mill, all of which means that a visit to Mount Vernon is really an all-day affair for first-time visitors.

The layers of history to experience at Mount Vernon go on. Inside the twenty-one-room house, special items, such as the key to the Bastille, which was given to Washington by the Marquis de Lafayette himself, hang in the central hall. New wallpapers and decorative paint finishes are valuable objects that are admired by some visitors. A favorite activity for visitors is to finish the house tour and sit on the piazza in stationary Chippendale-style chairs directly facing the Potomac River. A large swath of green grass frames the view, and boats with bright-white sails pass. For a fraction of a moment, this view is a step back in time.

The museum and education center on site has another 9,500 objects in its collection, some of which are brought out for changing exhibits. Films, text panels and more examine Washington, his family, the enslaved community and Washington's role in the French and Indian War, the American Revolution and the founding of a new nation.

Others prefer to visit the enslaved persons' memorial on site, which is a walk through a forested landscape, down past George and Martha Washington's tombs. The gravesites of the enslaved have received more attention in the past few years, as ground-penetrating radar has helped archaeologists identify burial sites without disturbing the remains. Many enslaved individuals did not have formal grave markers, further obfuscating the location and information of each burial. The work is ongoing, and a brief memorial service is held every day. This is likewise true for Washington's tomb, as a brief service is also held in the brick courtyard of the tomb area every morning and afternoon.

Like some of his age, Washington was opposed to the idea of slavery—of keeping humans in bondage—but he practiced it daily and only freed one man, William Lee, his personal butler, upon his own death. Washington favored gradual abolition, which, in essence, kicked the can down the curb for future generations to work out. It took another great war, the Civil War, to do this. Make sure you pick up the special "Enslaved People of Mount Vernon Map & Guide," which will help you understand the close relationship between white owners and overseers and the Black enslaved laborers. Their daily lives and the places they lived and worked were intertwined—which is the very name of a podcast series produced by staff of the Washington Library at Mount Vernon (https://www.georgewashingtonpodcast.com/show/intertwined-the-enslaved-community-at-george-washingtons-mount-vernon-1/). Mount Vernon provides a stunning comparison in terms of where people slept and how they lived, as a re-created barracks-style quarters, rebuilt in the 1950s, exists, hidden behind the greenhouse. The contrast between the Mansion House and the bunkhouse is stark.

Visitors can extend their stay at Mount Vernon by taking a ferry ride on the Potomac River, which travels north to Washington, D.C., to view (from the boat) the major memorials, including the Lincoln Memorial, the Jefferson Memorial and, of course, the Washington Monument (this author wrote the Washington Library encyclopedia entry for the monument, which you can read here, https://www.mountvernon.org/library/digitalhistory/digital-encyclopedia/article/washington-monument/). Mount Vernon runs a highly active year-round programming schedule. You can walk down to the wharf and just enjoy the view and then travel up the pathway to the Pioneer Farm, an unusual experiment that re-creates the kinds of agricultural activities that Washington developed and employed. A standalone re-created slave cabin is located here, as well as a re-created treading barn for wheat.

The basic areas to visit when you come to Mount Vernon are the mansion and, on the grounds, the blacksmith shop, slave quarters, outbuildings, gardens, pioneer farm, Washington tomb, the Slave Memorial and Cemetery and the wharf. A full-on Revolutionary War weekend in early May, a Fourth of July event and a Christmas candlelight tour are some of the property's largest annual programs, with food always available on site at the museum's café, which has indoor and outdoor seating. Finish your visit there, or get some sustenance at the Mount Vernon Inn Restaurant, located on the grounds of Mount Vernon, which serves colonial-inspired foods, such as hoe cakes and peanut soup.

Purple Heart Monument
Mount Vernon Estate
Mount Vernon Memorial Highway

Know anyone in your family who is the recipient of a Purple Heart? This special medal, created by George Washington during the American Revolution, continues to be awarded for bravery under fire. There is a Purple

The Purple Heart Monument located near the entrance to George Washington's Mount Vernon.

Heart monument close to the entrance to Mount Vernon, and all Purple Heart winners receive a free entry ticket. A small granite standing stone dedicated to the history of this unique American award can be found here. These monuments can also be found in communities across the country, connecting veterans and their service to the first commander in chief of the American army. A portion of the Mount Vernon Memorial Highway is also known as a "Purple Heart Trail," the signs for which are placed on lampposts near the exterior brick walls of the Mount Vernon Estate.

Ona Judge (circa 1773–1848) Historical Marker
Mount Vernon Estate
Mount Vernon Memorial Highway

One of the newest locations of public history in Alexandria and South Fairfax County, this historical marker was dedicated on Juneteenth in 2021, the first Juneteenth celebrated as a federal holiday in the United States. Placed diagonally across the street from the entrance to Mount Vernon, the marker is close to the Washington–Rochambeau Route Historical Marker and Wayside. Ona Judge's history was popularized by professor and author Erica Armstrong Dunbar, who wrote *Never Caught: The Washingtons' Relentless Pursuit of Their Runaway Slave, Ona Judge* (New York: Simon & Schuster, 2018), a finalist for the National Book Award. The story of Ona or "Oney" Judge is one of resistance against the enslavement carried out by the Washingtons, both Martha and George. This historical marker, one of the first in a new program from the Virginia Department of Historic Resources highlighting Black history, was proposed and worked on by students in the Fairfax County School System. The marker reads:

> Ona (or Oney) Judge, born into slavery at Mount Vernon, became Martha Washington's personal attendant as a child. After George Washington was elected president in 1789, Judge was brought to New York City and later to Philadelphia to serve his household. Washington periodically sent her back to Virginia to skirt a Pennsylvania law that might have granted her freedom based on long-term residency. In 1796, after learning that she was to become a gift for Martha Washington's granddaughter, Judge escaped from Philadelphia to New Hampshire. There, she married and had three children, taught herself to read and write and lived for more than 50 years, having resisted Washington's attempts to recover her.

Washington–Rochambeau Route Marker and Wayside
Mount Vernon Estate
Mount Vernon Memorial Highway

There are several historical markers in the city of Alexandria and farther afield in South Fairfax County delineating the local path of George Washington and the Comte de Rochambeau on what is now called the Washington–Rochambeau Revolutionary Route. Traveling from Newport, Rhode Island, the Continental army, under the command of Washington and Rochambeau, marched 680 miles south, meeting with Lafayette and his forces in Virginia, where they joined as one to confront Cornwallis, the British general, at Yorktown, Virginia, in the last months of 1781. The French navy had already provided the Americans with a victory over the British navy in the Battle of the Chesapeake, leaving Cornwallis without reinforcements. He surrendered, marking the end of the American Revolutionary War. The marker at Mount Vernon gives visitors much to think about regarding Washington—that he was away from his home, plantation and family for eight years of war. The marker reads, "General Washington, in 1781, rode 60 miles in one day from Baltimore to Mount Vernon, which he had not visited in over 6 years. General Rochambeau arrived next day with his and

The Washington-Rochambeau Historic Marker, located across from the entrance to George Washington's Mount Vernon.

Washington's staff. They spent Sept. 10 and 11 at Mount Vernon before going on to Fredericksburg." You can also find a Washington–Rochambeau Route Virginia Historical Highway Marker in the city of Alexandria, directly across the street from the Lee-Fendall House, and you can find another in Colchester in Fairfax County.

Mount Vernon Distillery and Gristmill
5514 Mount Vernon Memorial Highway
Alexandria, VA 22309
www.mountvernon.org/the-estate-gardens/distillery-gristmill

Located three miles from Mount Vernon proper (the remaining land enclosed by red-brick walls, a design feature created in the twentieth century) is another historical site, this one dedicated to Washington's gristmill and distillery. The Virginia Department of Historic Resources placed a series of highway markers across the street, one of which is dedicated to the gristmill, reading:

In 1771, George Washington replaced a deteriorated gristmill that his father, Augustine, may have erected as early as the 1730s. The new mill ground grain from Mount Vernon and neighboring farms and was outfitted with two pairs of millstones. In 1791, Washington installed improvements that had recently been developed and patented by Oliver Evans of Delaware. Other structures at the site included a stone whiskey distillery, a malthouse, a cooperage, a miller's cottage and slave quarters. Washington's mill was razed around 1850, and in 1933, the Commonwealth of Virginia built a reconstruction on the original site.

There is a free shuttle from Mount Vernon and a parking lot if you want to drive yourself. Here, you can tour three buildings and witness a massive water wheel turn; it ground corn and other grains grown in Washington's time for profit and personal use. Most people know Washington had a sweet tooth, eating hoe cakes or corn cakes every morning with butter and honey, see www.mountvernon.org/inn/recipes/article/hoecakes for the recipe. In the second stone building on site, visitors can see the large wooden barrels

The interior of George Washington's distillery, a replica of his profitable business.

that contain the newest whiskies produced in the stills in the basement. All the products created here can be purchased in the shop on site, with the whiskies selling out every year due to limited production.

Across the busy street are three more Virginia Department of Historic Resources Highway Markers, each giving viewers more contextual history of this part of South Fairfax County.

DOEG INDIGENOUS PEOPLE

Not surprisingly, since the area is dotted with water sources, such as creeks, and its proximity to the Potomac River, Indigenous people first traveled through the area during the prehistoric era, hunting and foraging. Eventually, as recounted in this historic marker sign, a community called the Doeg, semi-settled Indigenous people, came into contact with the English settlers. Many Indigenous place names were utilized by the British in North America; nearby, George Washington purchased land, a portion of which was called Dogue Run Farm, which became one of his five plantations and eight thousand acres. More information about the Doeg is provided on the historic highway marker:

> *A group of Virginia Indians referred to as the Doeg (but also Dogue, Taux, and other names) occupied villages and settlements along the Potomac and Occoquan Rivers by 1607. They included Tauxenant, near Mount Vernon, and Assaomeck, near Alexandria. The Doeg lived a semi-sedentary lifestyle that involved farming and extended hunting and fishing trips. The English forced many of the Doeg out of this region by the late 17th century. Nearby Dogue Creek is named for them.*

Muddy Hole Farm Park
7941 Kidd Street
Alexandria, VA 22309
www.fairfaxcounty.gov/parks

Drive into the parking lot at Muddy Hole Farm Park today, and you could be forgiven for thinking the green space here has perhaps always looked like this. Wide-open fields, a basketball court and a couple of picnic tables suggest a quiet neighborhood park in the middle of suburbia. Muddy

Muddy Hole Farm Park, one of the five farms owned by George Washington.

Hole, which now has a concrete culvert running through it to channel water, was once one of George Washington's five farms that, together, composed his Mount Vernon Plantation. George Mason once owned part of this land, which, eventually, Washington purchased as he grew his land holdings. Plantation landscapes such as this had agricultural fields that were worked by enslaved men, women and children. There were forty-six enslaved people who lived and worked here, including nineteen children. The beginning of the farm was much like those of Washington's other farm sites; it was started as a tobacco farm, which was phased out for other cash crops due to the depleted soil. According to museum staff, other crops in rotation here included hemp. The story of Muddy Hole Farm in Washington's time was documented in ledger books and other documents Washington kept. Without any interpretation on site from the Fairfax County Park Authority, the current manager of the park, your best bet is to drive to the site and read the history provided by George Washington's Mount Vernon on your smartphone. Visit www.mountvernon.org/library/ digitalhistory/digital-encyclopedia/article/muddy-hole-farm and try to imagine the past.

Grist Mill Park

4710 Mount Vernon Memorial Highway
Alexandria, VA 22309
www.fairfaxcounty.gov/parks/grist-mill-park-master-plan-revision

Owned by the Fairfax County Park Authority, Grist Mill Park preserves a twentieth-century barn and silo, making a great contrast to the barns and silos you may have just seen at George Washington's Mount Vernon. The community park today is the place for planned recreational activities, such as soccer games, and it contains a large and very active dog park. During the summer, "Mount Vernon Nights" are held at Grist Mill Park with live music.

The other historical marker here tells visitors that they are transitioning out of the Mount Vernon area as we know it today and into another neighborhood with many historical sites. Not surprisingly, many places are related to George Washington, as his reach in the Alexandria area was both wide and deep. But this area is also well known for the Black community that developed here out of a long relationship between Washington, Mount Vernon and free

Grist Mill Park in the Alexandria section of Fairfax County, a twentieth-century dairy farm.

and enslaved Black Americans. The descendants of that community and the contemporary families who work, live and contribute to this place remember their heritage and history in the Gum Springs neighborhood.

Gum Springs Historical Society/Gum Springs Museum and Cultural Center
Gum Springs Community Center
8100 Fordson Road
Alexandria, VA 22306
www.gumspringsmuseum.blogspot.com

In this area of the world, the name George Washington is currency. But if you add the name West Ford to the Washington family legacy, you begin to see how Black Americans made their lives and fortunes in and out of bondage, often on the landscapes where many once labored. Entrepreneurship, family and faith are at the center of many such histories, but the story of West Ford is a standout, because so much is known about him. In addition, he was photographed on the site of his former enslavement, Mount Vernon. His story is a rare and insightful look into the lives of freed Black Americans just after the Civil War. Wes, or West, Ford was born into slavery and was therefore the possession of the Bushrod Washington, George Washington's nephew and the owner, in the early nineteenth century, of Mount Vernon.

Bushrod was the Washington who gained ownership of Mount Vernon after George and Martha's deaths in, respectively, 1799 and 1801. Ford was freed when Bushrod himself died in 1829, attesting to the great respect and relationship Bushrod and his wife felt toward the man who had served the family and their businesses in multiple roles. The relationship between Bushrod Washington and West Ford was likely closer than simply one of respect; Wes was either the son of Bushrod, Bushrod's father or one of his brothers. West Ford was the son of Venus, a woman who was first enslaved on a Virginian plantation in Westmorland County. Forced sexual relationships were a part of the egregious practices of enslavement.

Later in life, as an older, sickly man, Ford returned to Mount Vernon for care under the Mount Vernon Ladies' Association, the group of women who came to own and preserve the house. Ford was then photographed on the grounds of Mount Vernon. You can read more about him and see his image through the Digital Encyclopedia of George Washington via Mount Vernon:

The exterior of the Gum Springs Historical Society/Gum Springs Museum and Cultural Center.

www.mountvernon.org/library/digitalhistory/digital-encyclopedia/article/ west-ford.

In addition to his emancipation, Bushrod left Ford 160 acres of land, which provided economic influence and stability, enabling the freed man to begin a life of entrepreneurship and activity when he sold the land and bought a larger tract. West founded the town of Gum Springs just a few years later, in 1833, which became a site for those who were formerly enslaved to gather, build together and restart life independent of the slave system, which was still the norm in Virginia and the rest of the South. Other early Black settlers included Samuel Taylor, a self-emancipated man who established the Bethlehem Baptist Church in Gum Springs. A group of Quakers helped the community establish its first school. Because of this early history, Gum Springs is known today as the oldest Black community in Fairfax County and is currently the subject of a potential Historic District Study, which will more fully document the "innovations and self-sufficiencies" of the community. Today, around five hundred descendants still live in the Gum Springs area.

WOODLAWN CULTURAL LANDSCAPE HISTORIC DISTRICT

The last historical marker found outside Mount Vernon's gristmill is the marker for the Woodlawn Historic District. Driving just a mile from here, you come to a crossing. Here, where the Washington Memorial Parkway ends, is a modern crossroads of sorts, where a left turn takes you to the Woodlawn Historic District and farther along to Fort Belvoir, and a right turn takes you into the Mount Vernon neighborhood, a dense area of housing, restaurants, gas stations and needed amenities. Drive straight ahead, and you head toward Kingstowne and the Hayfield area of Alexandria. It is a mix of the residential and the commercial with some open areas of Virginia landscape. Each of the sites is discussed further in this section, after this succinct summary of the area:

> *This 152-acre historic district was part of George Washington's Mount Vernon estate. In 1789, Washington gave the Woodlawn tract to his stepdaughter Eleanor Parke Custis and her husband, Lawrence Lewis. Northern Quakers bought the property in 1846 and sold parcels to white and free African American farmers. The historic district includes the Lewises' Woodlawn mansion (ca. 1805), the Quakers' meetinghouse and burial ground, and a cemetery established by Woodlawn Methodist Church, an African American congregation. Also preserved here are George Washington's gristmill, reconstructed in 1933, and the Frank Lloyd Wright–designed Pope-Leighey House, completed in 1941 and moved here in 1965.*

Quaker Meeting House
Alexandria Friends Meeting at Woodlawn
8990 Woodlawn Road
Alexandria, VA 22309
www.woodlawnfriends.org/home

The Quaker Meeting House is a traditional, simple, wood-frame building that still serves its active community of "Friends." Quaker values espouse simplicity in architecture, and this is sometimes called "Quaker Plain style." Walk behind the building to see a historic graveyard, including a mound of grave markers. The Quakers here have a long history of working toward equality. The area's settlers came from Pennsylvania, New York and New

The exterior of the Woodlawn Quaker Meeting House, located near Woodlawn Plantation House.

Jersey to establish a new community in which Black and white people could live and work together in order to create economic independence for all.

Woodlawn
9000 Richmond Highway
Alexandria, VA 22309
www.woodlawnpopeleighey.org

Woodlawn Mansion was originally part of George Washington's 8,000-acre plantation and is now a National Historic Landmark. At Woodlawn, there are 126 acres of open land remaining, and the house has undergone a significant reinterpretation by its owner, the National Trust for Historic Preservation. This house was, in fact, the first property ever owned by the National Trust, and this, in combination with its direct association to George Washington and Mount Vernon, indicates why the house is listed as a National Historic Landmark, the highest designation of historical significance for buildings in the United States.

The exterior of the Woodlawn Plantation, the first property owned by the National Trust for Historic Preservation.

Woodlawn Plantation was finished around 1805 as a wedding gift of land and property from George Washington to Eleanor Parke "Nelly" Custis and her new husband, Lawrence Lewis. Custis was Martha Washington's granddaughter who grew up at Mount Vernon, and Lewis was Washington's nephew, so the ties were strong between these two families. The 6,500-square-foot house was designed by Dr. William Thornton, who is remembered today as the architect of the U.S. Capitol. Washington called the place "a most beautiful site for a gentleman's seat," and like they did at Mount Vernon, many guests came to stay at Woodlawn for extended periods. But the fact is, Virginians' hospitality was based on the labor of enslaved people, who cared for everyone in the house, resident and visitor alike. At Woodlawn, this meant the work of ninety enslaved men, women and children between the house and the plantation.

Eventually, the house passed out of the ownership of the Lewis family and was purchased by the Quakers, who had the idea to create a farming community intended to demonstrate the possibility that farmers, both Black and white, could live and work together in the same community. For decades they were committed to this work, even through the Civil War, which devastated the community. Their concept of a "free labor"–type of community lasted into the early twentieth century. By that time, the Quakers had built their own, less-ostentatious meetinghouse close by, and many of the original settlers and their families moved away.

Pope-Leighey House
9000 Richmond Highway
Alexandria, VA 22309
www.woodlawnpopeleighey.org

On the grounds of Woodlawn is another historic house, this one of a decidedly more modern vintage style. The Pope-Leighey House is a special treat for visitors to Alexandria. It is the only Frank Lloyd Wright House open to the public in the DMV. Smaller than the average historic house museum, the house offered ingenious solutions to modern living. Donated to the National Trust for Historic Preservation in 1965, the house was

The exterior of the Pope-Leighey House, designed by Frank Lloyd Wright.

moved to the Woodlawn Plantation site due to the threat of demolition for the creation of I-66 through Falls Church, Virginia. Fortunately, Woodlawn, the National Trust's first historic house property, was close by, and the landscape, full of trees, shrubs and natural flora, was a good match to the original house site.

The house is small by today's standards: 1,200 square feet for two bedrooms, a living room/den, a kitchen and a bath, but it seems much bigger when stepping inside. Its tall ceilings, large windows—some floor-to-ceiling—and open spaces create the illusion that the space is larger than it is. Interior decoration is kept to a minimum; instead, the windows invite the outside in. Additionally, Wright used a cut-out, geometric design along the "gallery," or upper window story, of the house, which almost seems like a secret code of some sort and/or harkens back the ancient world, when pictographs provided stories lost in time. The furniture is original to the house and features cleverly made side chairs that slot together like pieces of a 3D puzzle.

Frank Lloyd Wright's vision for Usonian architecture was centered here on affordability, crafty solutions to longstanding housing problems and the application of new materials in unexpected ways. For example, although the house has almost no insulation, the temperature is comfortable, even in colder Virginia weather. This is because Wright placed radiant heat under the home's concrete floors. Storage cabinets are placed behind walls so as not to detract from the smoothness of the wood. On one side, one of Wright's famous cantilevers extends out from the house proper, with its center cut out, leaving a space for viewing clouds as they pass overhead. The house is sheathed in cypress siding, while the inside features red brick in addition to wood walls. The house dates to around 1940 but would be pleasant to live in even today.

Arcadia Center for Sustainable Food and Agriculture
9000 Richmond Highway
Alexandria, VA 22309
http://www.arcadiafood.org

Arcadia is a not-for-profit organization located on land owned by the National Trust for Historic Preservation as part of the Woodlawn/Pope-Leighey Historic Site. Bringing forward the relationship between historic houses and historic working landscapes, Arcadia has a mission to connect

Active beehives at the Arcadia Center for Sustainable Food and Agriculture, a partnership and part of the Woodlawn-Pope-Leighey House's historic landscape owned by the National Trust for Historic Preservation.

people to farming, especially military veterans and school-age students, all the while growing food for communities in need in the District of Columbia and surrounding areas. Although the working farm is not open for visitors due to the pandemic, rest assured the honeybees are doing well in their hives. Mount Vernon currently has nine hives in operation, and even the Kennedy Center in Washington, D.C., keeps beehives on its roof. Although honeybees were brought to the American colonies in 1620, making them some of the earliest passengers (they were needed to make honey as a sweetener), today, the primary purpose of bee keepers of all sizes is to support pollination, since two-thirds of the world's crops depend on bees. The importance of honeybees is evident by the fact that the Commonwealth of Virginia keeps on staff a state apiarist. At Mount Vernon, honeybees pollinate many crops, including squash.

Potomac Heritage National Scenic Trail
Richmond Highway
Alexandria, VA
www.nps.gov/pohe/index

Located at the back entrance to Woodlawn, at the intersection of Richmond Highway and Jeff Todd Way, is a corner that exemplifies the past and present melding together. Two corners of the intersection are commercial property (a gas station and a Roy Rogers, and both are always busy), while the other two corners of the intersection remain rural with some agriculture and landscaping. The Potomac Heritage National Scenic Trail passes through here, and though the traffic is heavy most of the time, bikers made good use of the paved trail that connects Fairfax County with multiple points, including the Mount Vernon Trail, the Northern Neck Heritage Trail, the C&O Canal Towpath and the George Washington Memorial Parkway. At this intersection is a walking entrance to Woodlawn/Pope-Leighey House, and farther along the trail, there is a historic farmstead (not open to the public) that is currently under a slow process of restoration.

An interpretive sign and map for the Potomac Heritage National Scenic Trail, Richmond Highway.

The Woodlawn Historic District is, in fact, surrounded by Fort Belvoir, a fenced 8,658-acre historic and contemporary army fort with fifty thousand employees (military and civilian) located on land that once belonged to the Fairfax family. Although you can enter the base as a visitor, Fort Belvoir has recently opened a brand-new museum on a publicly accessible area of the base, which might be enough to satisfy your curiosity about the U.S. Army, past and present. Driving through this area of South Fairfax County, with its open vistas of Virginian landscape, it is easy to forget that you are only thirty minutes south of the U.S. capital.

U.S. Army Fort Belvoir
Tulley Gate / Pence Gate
9500 Pohick Road
Fort Belvoir, VA 22060
home.army.mil/belvoir/index.php/about/Garrison/DES/physical-security/
installation-accessgates/expedited-visitor-access-service

From the Virginia Department of Historical Markers comes the following information about historic Fort Belvoir, emphasizing it as the home of the U.S. Army Corps of Engineers:

> *Fort Belvoir is named for the 18th-century plantation that was owned by William Fairfax. The house burned in 1783. The U.S. War Department acquired much of the Belvoir tract in 1912 as a training center and named it Camp A.A. Humphreys for Maj. Gen. Andrew A. Humphreys, a former chief of engineers. During World War I, the camp was enlarged, and the Engineer School was moved here. The fort was renamed Fort Humphreys in 1922. In 1935, President Franklin D. Roosevelt changed the name to Fort Belvoir. The Engineer School moved to Fort Leonard Wood, Mo., in 1988.*

So, what is missing from this historic marker, installed on site of Pence Gate, one of seven access points to the Fort, in 1998? Today, in 2021, the U.S. Army is rethinking the names of many installations and bases across the United States in response to the recognition that many are named for men who were racist and/or practiced racist policies in their work. You wouldn't know it from the historic marker, but Fort Belvoir falls into this category, as explained by Ty Seidule, professor emeritus of history at West Point. In his 2020 book, *Robert E. Lee and Me, A Southerner's Reckoning with the Lost Cause* (New York: Macmillan, 2021), Seidule, who grew up in Alexandria, explains that the original name for the Fort, Humphreys, was a good choice, since he was a "stellar Civil War U.S. general and one of the finest engineers of the nineteenth century."

What made President Franklin Delano Roosevelt change the name over to Belvoir, which Seidule says refers to the plantation house owned by Thomas Fairfax, the sixth Lord Fairfax of Cameron and great friend to close neighbor George Washington? At the time of the American Revolution, the Fairfax family, deeply Loyalist—Fairfax was "the only British peer to settle in America"—returned to England and eventually went bankrupt. In the 1930s, the foundations of the manor house were found again in the woods, and to curry favor with a white supremacist from Alexandria named Howard W. Smith, who also happened to be a congressman and in the House Committee on Rules, a powerful entity within Congress, Seidule suggests that Roosevelt allowed the name change so that Smith would continue to vote for his proposed progressive legislation.

As discussed in the preface of this book, name changes across the city of Alexandria, as well as in South Fairfax County, continue, and the U.S. Army continues its own critical look inward. There is a Visitor Control Center open from 6:00 a.m. to 6:00 p.m. on weekdays, although the center was closed for much of the pandemic. When open, visitors will need a current "starred" license, and note that waiting times to obtain a pass can be long. If you manage to get on base, you can find the historic site that lent Fort Belvoir its name.

BELVOIR MANSION HISTORIC AREA

After you get through the check-in point at the Tulley Gate, as a visitor, you will have to pull off to enter the visitor center. There, you will show your driver's license and receive a pass for the day. Once back in your car, continue on Pohick Road and take a right at the intersection of Pohick and Gunston Roads. Drive south toward Fairfax Village, one of the housing developments for military families. Once you arrive at Fairfax Village, you will see a community center and a parking lot on your left. There are a few spaces reserved for visitors to the Belvoir Mansion Historic Area. Park here and walk toward the introductory text panel. Follow the one-mile trail and read the interpretation signage along the way. Once you reach a clearing,

The Belvoir Mansion Historic Site on the grounds of Fort Belvoir.

you must try to imagine that this wooded area was cleared for the mansion house, which would have had a view of the Potomac River below.

Belvoir Mansion was the result of an original land grant from King Charles II to his English supporters in North America. The marriage between a daughter of Lord Culpeper and Thomas, the fifth Lord Fairfax, resulted in this piece of property being inherited by their son, who moved to Virginia. The place on the Potomac River was named Belvoir, meaning "beautiful view," and a manor house was constructed on the site in 1741. The place remained the home of Thomas Fairfax until 1773, when stirrings of the American Revolution were on the horizon. A large plantation grew up around the manor house with equal parts agricultural and fishing spaces, all of which were worked by enslaved Black men, women and children. An advertisement for the rental of Belvoir Plantation, which ran in the *Virginia Gazette* in 1774, brings the house into focus:

> *To be RENTED, from year to year, or for a term of years, BELVOIR, the beautiful seat of Honorable George William Fairfax, Esq., lying upon Potowmack [sic] in Fairfax County, about fourteen miles below Alexandria. The mansion house is of brick, two stories high, with four convenient rooms*

and a large passage on the lower floor, five rooms and a passage on the second, and a servants' hall and cellars below, convenient offices, stables, and coach house adjoining, as also a large and well-furnished garden, stored with a great variety of valuable fruits, in good order. Appertaining to the tract on which these houses stand, and which contain near 2000 acres (surrounding in a manner navigable by water) are several valuable fisheries, and a good deal of cleared land in different parts.

The home was destroyed by a fire in 1783. Although there are no surviving drawings of the house, archaeologists found plenty of evidence of the home in the earth, including household goods, such a ceramics, glass and metal utensils for eating. The land eventually passed out of the hands of descendants and was purchased by the United States government in 1910, becoming Camp A.A. Humphreys in 1918. A small family cemetery still exists on the site with an obelisk monument dedicated to the Fairfax family. Beyond the manor house site, which is delineated in the grass with an outline of stones, there is a trail that winds along the Potomac River with a natural history interpretation.

Thermo-Con House

Another historic house site is part of Fort Belvoir, although this one is decidedly more modern. A still-in-use "Thermo-Con" house was built in the residential section of the military base, a unique preservation "save" from the U.S. Army more in the line with the International Modernism espoused by Frank Lloyd Wright's Pope-Leighey House than the eighteenth-century plantations of Belvoir, Woodlawn and Mount Vernon. The historic sign provided by the fort tells you what you always wanted to know about a Thermo-Con house:

In 1948, the Department of Defense worked with Higgins Industries to develop a standard house design to meet the army's housing shortage. Higgins industries designed and mass-produced landing craft during World War II and held the patent for "Thermo-Con," a cement material that expanded as it cured. The renowned industrial architects, Albert Kahn and Associates, designed the prototype in the International style and the 410th Engineer Battalion (construction) completed the building in 1949. Due to its innovative design and construction techniques, the house was placed on

The exterior of the Thermo-Con House at Fort Belvoir.

the Virginia Landmarks Register in 1997. In 2000, the army renovated and returned "Thermo-Con" house to use as a distinguished visitor housing.

Before leaving base, there are other historic artifacts to be seen, including a large piece of an original column from the U.S. Treasury building in Washington, D.C.

National Museum of the United States Army
1775 Liberty Drive
Fort Belvoir, VA 22060
www.armyhistory.org

The U.S. Army has a strong history and identity attached to this area of Virginia. The army was created by the Second Continental Congress on June 14, 1775, and George Washington was immediately put in charge as commander in chief. So, the army is almost 250 years old and will celebrate its semiquincentennial in 2025 (the following year, in 2026, the United States will celebrate its semiquincentennial, see www.america250.org). On the

An exhibit featuring World War I at the Museum of the U.S. Army at Fort Belvoir.

grounds of Fort Belvoir, the large army base located close to Mount Vernon, a brand-new museum opened in November 2020 to commemorate this long history, a history especially focused on the experiences of the American soldier. Several pandemic-related delays marred the full opening of the museum, but the crowds come anyway. Tickets are free but must be reserved ahead of time; the parking is plentiful and also free. The modernist building gleams in the Virginia sun. Interpretation and storytelling begin before you enter the building, with signposts depicting contemporary soldiers and their service stories along the path to the entrance.

Inside the museum are a series of large galleries divided chronologically, from the "Founding the Nation" Gallery to the "Cold War" and "Changing World" Galleries. The War on Terror is depicted, as with many of the exhibits in the galleries, with life-sized army figures in action. Thus, in the "Nation Overseas" Gallery, visitors can walk through an immersive lighting and sound show depicting World War I soldiers and trench warfare. Real guns, tanks and even an authentic Higgins assault boat—one of six known to have landed at Normandy on D-Day—and an iconic UH-1B "Huey" helicopter used in Vietnam provide a small visual sliver of what active duty was like for generations of American soldiers.

One of the areas not yet finished at the museum is the Medal of Honor Experience and Garden. The garden is an outdoor exhibit that reinforces what visitors learn in the gallery space and offers a place for reflection about the meaning of the highest medal of valor the army bestows on select soldiers. In addition, there is an experiential learning center for those with a desire to pilot aircraft and other machines of war (at cost) and an army theater that shows the film *Of Noble Deeds* on a three-hundred-degree screen. Finally, in true museum fashion, there is a gift shop and an onsite café with drinks and snacks.

Huntley Meadows Park
Norma Hoffman Visitor Center
3701 Lockheed Boulevard
Alexandria, VA 22306
www.fairfaxcounty.gov/parks/huntley-meadows-park

Huntley Meadows is a huge draw for nature lovers and naturalists. People come from across Northern Virginia to visit the unique wetlands here, known for its spectacular bird, amphibian and insect life. Huntley Meadows appears as a green area on your Google Map; it is really the last "natural" preserve of this size in Alexandria and often becomes a way station for unique wildlife observations. In the summer of 2021, for example, three bright-pink roseate spoonbills, a bird that adopted Huntley Meadows, made an unlikely appearance and became the subject of photographers' lenses. One spoonbill appeared and then another, and soon, there were three, delighting visitors of all ages. Naturalist photographers set up shop early in the day, placing their cameras on the boardwalks and sharing wildlife views and information with visitors. Earlier in the year, a family of Madagascar ducks were popular to watch, and the numerous beavers are always a favorite with the crowds. Great blue herons and egrets are common. If you own a pair of binoculars, Huntley Meadows is the place to use them.

Dogs are allowed in the park up to the boardwalk. From there, a boardwalk circles, cuts through and edges around the marshlands of Huntley Meadows, allowing close views of box, painted and snapping turtles; frogs; butterflies and moths; and birds, such as red-winged blackbirds, cardinals, wrens and even bald eagles (the wetlands are not far from the Potomac River, where many bald eagles live and nest). Snakes, toads and insects are also common creatures at Huntley Meadows. Most locals or regular visitors will tell you

The exterior of the Norma Hoffman Visitor Center at Huntley Meadows Park.

their favorite part about the park is its seasonally changing natural landscape. Every visit brings a new "scene" as grasses and flowers grow and then die off. Huntley Meadows is never the same place twice. The visitor center, closed for much of the pandemic, is now reopened and contains excellent exhibits on the people who made every effort to save Huntley Meadows after the land was relinquished by the federal government at the end of the Cold War.

How did this natural area in the Hybla Valley get its name? Continue reading to find out.

Historic Huntley
6918 Harrison Lane
Alexandria, VA 22306
www.fairfaxcounty.gov/parks/historic-huntley

Most Alexandrians know the name Huntley Meadows, recognizable for its natural landscape and the wildlife viewing there, but fewer people know that the park was named for the historic house located close by. Historic

Huntley is today surrounded by residential housing developments and busy roads, but the area began life as a plantation. The land was first owned by George Mason IV, the grandson of George Mason (of Gunston Hall) and was inherited by his grandson Thomson Francis Mason. This Mason was the mayor of Alexandria from 1827 to 1830. He built a "villa"-style country residence outside of the city proper and added outbuildings around the property, including a "necessary" (bathroom), an icehouse, a tenant's house and storage areas. Built of red bricks painted bright yellow, Historic Huntley was purchased and renovated by the Fairfax County Park Authority in 1989.

A rather new addition to the park's holdings in Northern Virginia, it would take more than a decade of preservation work to stabilize the historic architecture, and the house finally opened its doors in 2012. The Friends of Historic Huntley opens the historic house during the summer season on the weekends and provides special night visit programs, tours focused on the enslaved people who worked here and scout programs. The house is perched on a hill, overlooking the Hybla Valley below, and it is listed in the National Register of Historic Places, the Virginia Landmarks Register and the Fairfax County Historic House Inventory. Although the house is only partially furnished, there are enough objects in the central passage to

The interior of Historic Huntley, showcasing a mantelpiece with family photographs.

suggest the refinement of the house's architecture and the way it would have looked in the nineteenth century. As with many park sites, the grounds are open from dawn to dusk, and picnic tables are available, along with exterior interpretive signage.

Carolltown Historic Marker

Intersection of Kingstowne Village Parkway and Summer Ridge Road
Alexandria, VA 22315

There are many historic markers to be found along Virginia roads, streets, parkways and highways. This is because the commonwealth has placed a lot of effort into placing its black-and-white metal signs throughout the state over the course of the past one hundred years. You read that correctly—Virginia has been invested in documenting and sharing history for a very long time. Northern Virginia is particularly rich in doing local history because of the significance of its Revolutionary and Civil War sites; also, more entities have joined the Virginia Department of Historic Resources in placing roadway or highway markers. Since 1998, the Fairfax County History Commission, for example, has placed more than fifty of its own historic markers, including one in Carrolltown. The color of the Fairfax County Historic Markers, blue and buff, were drawn from George Washington's Virginia militia uniform and the uniform he continued to wear as commander in chief of the Continental army throughout the war and long after.

Historic highway markers are useful ways to share public history, especially for sites that no longer exist. A marker can help you envision what happened in a specific locale in the past and can provide clues to the marked development of urban areas, especially those like Carrolltown, which have changed completely from rural/agricultural areas to suburban areas. Today, standing in Kingstowne, a residential tract of more than five thousand apartments, condominiums and townhouses located on a bluff between West Alexandria and Springfield, you would never know, except for the historic markers and a few preserved historic sites of significance, about the lives and work of generations of people whose story may not be known but who greatly contributed to the growth of the area. The Carrolltown marker shares a bit of this history:

> In this vicinity, a small African American settlement grew from ten acres of land given to Jane Caroll by her owner, Dennis Johnston, before 1856.

The Carrolltown Historic Marker for the Black community in this area of Fairfax County.

Jane's son, George, acquired an additional 121 acres from Johnston's heirs in 1899 and 1903. In 1904, George Caroll sold approximately 50 acres to family members. In 1881 and 1884 William Jasper, a former slave of William Hayward Foote of Hayfield Farm, donated land for a school and the Laurel Grove Baptist Church on Beulah Street. A community grew around the school, church and a general store operated by George Carroll on the present-day Kingstowne Village Parkway.

Laurel Grove Colored School and Church

6840 Beulah Street
Alexandria, VA 22310
www.laurelgroveschool.org/index

Fortunately, one structure from the historic period of South Fairfax County still exists. Just a five-minute drive from the Carrolltown Historic Marker is the site of the Laurel Grove Colored School and Church. The schoolhouse

The exterior of the Laurel Grove Colored School and Church in southeast Fairfax County.

still stands, while the church building is long gone, although headstones in the small cemetery remain. The schoolhouse stands as a testament to the role of education in the lives of Alexandrians—Black and white—but also as a memory marker for a long era in American history, when Black students fought for the right to a full and equal education under the law. The small, white-sided building is commonly known as a "one-room schoolhouse," where students of various ages would study together. According to the community, the schoolhouse was closed in 1932 and restored by family descendants and interested citizens. Further, "Laurel Grove tells the unique story of a community's refusal to narrow its ambitions. Of all the 'colored' schools that opened in the region, only Laurel Grove exists today as a 'living museum.'" Laurel Grove Schoolhouse is surrounded by busy roadways and towering medical office buildings and commercial strips. The fact that it survives intact is an inspirational example of family and community organizers stepping up to save local history. Pull into the parking lot of the office building next door when visiting—spaces along the edge of the fence are reserved for visitors to the schoolhouse site.

Olander and Margaret Banks Neighborhood Park
7400 Old Telegraph Road
Alexandria, VA 22315
www.bankslegacy.org/copy-of-contact

Bringing the Carrolltown story into the mid-twentieth century, the following is an example of a small park—ten acres—with big impact. Located in a suburban development now called Kingstowne, in the mid-twentieth century, this open area was settled by Black families. The Banks purchased the open space in 1957, and Olander Banks, an entrepreneur, began building on the site. Today, what remains is the vestige of a lovely, walkable park, suitable for playing, picnicking and bird and nature watching. The red house with a gambrel roof remains; it was built by Banks for his nine children and looks deceptively small (there are twenty-seven rooms). Today, the site is owned by the Fairfax County Park Authority. Banks sold his home and property to the county, although he was able to live out the remainder of his life there. A large memorial to Olander and Margaret Banks was installed on the site by the family in 2005, who continue to visit the homestead today. The

The Olander and Margaret Banks Neighborhood Park Marker.

memorial features an inscription and two realistic portraits of the husband and wife on each side, always watching the activities happening in their park. The memorial marker reads:

> *This site is preserved in perpetuity as a park, thanks to the generosity of Mr. Olander Banks Sr., who dedicates it in memory of his wife, Margaret Lomax Banks. Olander Banks Sr. and Margaret L. Banks purchased this property in 1957. It was then an open gravel lot. Mrs. Banks suggested to her husband to use the vacant land to build a home at this site. Here, they built the 27-room home where they raised their nine children, and for over four decades, they made it a peaceful oasis for family and friends. In the face of intense surrounding development, Olander Banks Sr. was inspired to be "one with the dream" and share the estate with Fairfax County. The Fairfax County Park Authority established the Olander Banks Sr. and Margaret Lomax Banks Community Park in August 2001. Through his giving spirit and faith, Olander Banks Sr. has ensured that this will remain a special place for future generations to enjoy.*

Of great value to the small park is an unnamed tributary of Piney Branch Creek, which runs through the middle of the park, providing a waterway supporting abundant plant life and, in turn, supports birds and insects. There is also a secret place to investigate that is especially lovely in the spring. Banks must have been an avid gardener and landscaper in his time, because down a trail to a pool of water, cut stones create a pond where tadpoles spawn into frogs. *Plop, plop, plop.* You'll hear the frogs that jump into the water if you find this secret spot. Osage orange trees, redbuds and an old oak remain from a mixture of plantings, both old and new. Deer, fox, groundhogs and chipmunks can be observed.

The Fairfax County Park Authority owns several historic houses throughout the county, many in South Fairfax County, which are part of their park system. In order to have collaborations and help with maintenance and more, the park authority runs a "Resident Curator Program" that accepts applicants to specific open historic houses and expects, in return, that resident curators will put in the sweat equity to maintain and improve historic properties. The Banks House is in the Resident Curator Program. Because the house has not been renovated since the late twentieth century, there is much work to do. The program has proven a success for other historic sites—maybe it is just a matter of time before the right individual or organization sees the value in the Banks House and applies to become a resident curator.

Franconia Museum
Franconia Government Center
6121 Franconia Road
Alexandria, VA 22310
www.myrosehill.snappages.site

Close to Kingstowne and the original Carrolltown is an area of South Fairfax County called Franconia. Like many places, ask the residents of the area where the name of their town came from, and they will draw a blank. Historical markers such as this one remind residents and visitors that the ground on which they trod has been used by generations of people long before. Located on the grounds of the Franconia Government Center is the Franconia, Virginia Historic Marker that helps answer this question. The marker reads:

"Frankhonia Farm" was situated on 191 acres purchased in 1859 by Alexandria merchant and businessman William Fowle from Joseph Broders of Oak Grove Farm. His son, Robert Rollins Fowle, sold 18 acres to the Alexandria & Fredericksburg Railway Company in 1872 for

A Franconia Museum display case with publications.

163

a station, which was named after the farm. The station served as Garfield Post Office from 1881 to 1890 and again from 1898 to 1907. Initially situated south of Franconia Road near present-day Fleet Drive, the station was relocated after a fire in 1903 to the north side of Franconia Road. Regular service at Franconia Station was discontinued c. 1953.

But there is more to learn. Inside the Franconia Government Center is the one-room Franconia Museum. Residents of the area felt that their local history was important enough to share through this mini museum. Artifacts on display include Civil War uniforms, munitions from World War I and II and materials from local schools, people who lived in Franconia through the years and, from the outdoors, remembering Franconia's agricultural landscape, a plow.

Green Spring Gardens
4603 Green Spring Road
Alexandria, VA 22312
www.greenspring.org

Managed by the Fairfax County Park Authority, Green Spring Gardens is a small jewel in a densely packed residential and commercial area of Alexandria in the county. Saved from development due to the historic house on site, today, Green Spring Gardens has evolved into a horticulture center where plants can be purchased; there is also a recreational walking area with trails and different gardens on view and a special spot for weddings, a white gazebo overlooking a broad expanse of green lawn. The original inhabitants of the historic house would probably never have guessed the future in store for their plantation landscape. Today, the historic site/park is alive with programming, dog walkers and horticulture enthusiasts. During the pandemic, the staff at Green Spring created special programs in which boxed "high teas," that is, tea with small sandwiches and sweet treats, could be picked up and indulged in during a program on Zoom around different themes, such as women's history, food/culinary history and more.

You could have high tea, or you could learn about all things undercover by attending the "Secrets, Spies, Sputnik & Huntley" Program offered by the Fairfax County Park Authority. As it turns out, due to Alexandria's proximity to Washington, D.C., and the fact that it is in (and sometimes out of) Virginia, there is a long history of spycraft here, both during the

The exterior of Green Spring Gardens, managed by the Fairfax County Park Authority.

Civil War and Cold War eras. Northern Virginia parks have even served as drop sites for classified materials changing hands, as practiced by one of the most infamous spies of all, Robert Hanssen, who is currently serving fifteen consecutive life sentences. Unknown to the many daily visitors at Green Spring Park, this historic house also has a history of espionage. Michael Straight, a Cambridge-educated Americans became involved in the business during the years leading up to World War II. He worked for the Roosevelt and later the Kennedy administrations, serving as the deputy chairman of the National Endowment for the Arts, even though he had already confessed to working for the KGB earlier in his life. He had homes in Martha's Vineyard and Georgetown and owned Green Springs Farm, where he wrote his memoir, *On Green Spring Farm: The Life and Times of One Family in Fairfax County, Va., 1942–1966* (New York: Devon Press, 2004). The family later donated the house to Fairfax County.

9

MASON NECK AND LORTON

INTERSECTIONS OF NATIONAL HISTORY
AND NATURAL HISTORY

Pohick Episcopal Church
9301 Richmond Highway
Lorton, Virginia 22079
www.pohick.org

On this busy corner of Richmond Highway (Route 1) and Telegraph Road, where Pohick Episcopal Church sits, touting itself as "no steeple, but lots of people," there are a series of four Virginia Department of Historic Resource Markers, highlighting the most interesting bits of local lore tied to the church and this area of South Fairfax County. In the graveyard surrounding the church, there are numerous evocative early grave markers, including the oldest grave marker in Fairfax County, that of Lieutenant William Harris from 1698. Dating to the eighteenth century, there are fourteen markers belonging Revolutionary War patriots, and from the century after that, there are the graves of nine veterans of the War of 1812. A lone, small stone inscribed with "Long Tom Indian Chief" begs for more interpretation. Who was Long Tom, and why is he buried here? Local lore says that an "Indian chief" was shot and killed by a woman named Susanna Alexander, "either in self-defense or to save the life of her husband, John." The Alexander family is represented in this graveyard, relations of the John Alexander who founded the City of Alexandria. In addition, Washington and Rochambeau, who we met earlier in the book, passed through here on their way to Yorktown. This place has witnessed a lot of history, a taste of which is offered by the following markers.

The portal of the Pohick Episcopal Church in Lorton, Virginia.

POHICK CHURCH

The construction of this building was started in 1769 and completed by 1774, succeeding an earlier church that is located two miles to the south. It was the lower church of Truro Parish, established in 1732, the parish of Mount Vernon and Gunston Hall. George William Fairfax, George Washington and George Mason, vestrymen, were members of the building committee under which the church was constructed.

THE WASHINGTONS AT POHICK CHURCH

George Washington, like his father before him, served on the vestry of Truro Parish, which the Virginia General Assembly established in 1732. Colonial vestries managed parish affairs and provided crucial services to the community, including care for widows, orphans, the poor and the sick. Washington served several terms as church warden and is credited with leading the effort to replace Old Pohick Church, located about two miles south, with a new building that opened here in 1774. He donated the furnishings to the church and attended services here with his wife, Martha Dandridge Custis Washington, a devout Anglican. Their home, Mount Vernon, is located six miles to the east.

WILLIAM BROWN, MD (CIRCA 1748–1792)

Dr. William Brown, a Revolutionary War physician, was born in Scotland and raised in Maryland. After studying medicine at the University of Edinburgh, he established a practice in Alexandria. In 1775, he became a surgeon for the Second Virginia Regiment. In 1778, the Continental Congress appointed him physician general of the Middle Department, extending from the Hudson to the Potomac River. At the military hospital in Lititz, Brown compiled the "Lititz Pharmacopeia" (1778), a collection of medical procedures and formulas for the compounding of medications. This was the first American formulary and a pioneering effort to provide standardized care. Brown is buried here in Pohick Cemetery.

OLD TELEGRAPH LINE

One of the first telegraph lines in the world, a part of the Washington–New Orleans telegraph company, was built from Washington to Petersburg in 1847. From this, the road took its name.

MASON NECK

If you continue down Route 611 to Mason Neck, you will find a semirural area of the county that has remained without the large-scale housing developments that are endemic to much of Alexandria and Fairfax County. Surrounded by the waters of the Potomac River and Chesapeake Bay Watershed, you'll want to visit to get a breath of fresh air, away from the density of the urban sprawl and traffic. In Mason Neck, you'll find a mixture of historical and recreational opportunities.

As you drive into Mason Neck proper, the first historical things of note you will see are three Virginia Department of Historic Resources Markers on the ground of the Lewis Chapel/Cranford Memorial Methodist Church. This is a good place to pull off the road, stop and think about the ways in which early Virginia was settled by white Europeans of various nationalities, of their relationships to the Indigenous people who were here before them and how churches were central places of not only worship but also community life in rural areas. One of the markers is titled "Indian Attack," and though it is considered pejorative and prejudiced today, the words do bring to mind the often-tumultuous intermingling of different cultures and how these often-unbalanced, aggressive encounters became the standard treatment of Indigenous people, a legacy of injustice that the United States continues to grapple with.

LEWIS CHAPEL/CRANFORD MEMORIAL METHODIST CHURCH AND CEMETERY

This church is a combination of several structures built on the site of the first Pohick Church (1730–44), making this one of the earliest sites of a religious institution in Fairfax County. Lewis Chapel, named after a Methodist circuit rider, was built in 1857 and moved from a site nearby in 1952. Cranford Memorial, the main portion of the complex, was constructed in 1900.

INDIAN ATTACK

To the east, on Dogue Neck, "certain unknown Indians" attacked the house of Thomas Barton around 3:00 p.m. on Sunday, June 16, 1700, killing eight people with "arrowes & wooden tommahawkes [*sic*]." The neighboring Piscataway Indigenous people denied the attack and blamed the Wittowees. The Indigenous people involved were probably angered by the colonials' encroachment on their land and may have been encouraged by the French. Lieutenant Colonel George Mason wrote Governor Francis Nicholson that "this murder was the Horrablest that ever was" in present-day Fairfax County. Then part of Stafford County Mason increased the number of militia patrols, but the Indigenous people escaped.

Gunston Hall

10709 Gunston Road
Mason Neck, Virginia
www.gunstonhall.org

Calling itself the "home of American rights," Gunston Hall was the plantation and home of George Mason, a founding father and author of the Virginia Declaration of Rights. Gunston Hall is one of the many "founding fathers" homes located across Virginia, but his is perhaps the least well known of the group. The historic site, not far from Washington, D.C., but situated on the rural and recreational Mason Neck, feels a great distance away (likewise, George Mason's monument in Washington, D.C., located in the Tidal Basin area, is often overlooked). This lack of pressure from traffic and from hordes of pressing visitors is one of the charms of Gunston Hall. It must have been similar for Mason, who raised nine children there, with views of the water, land enough for a deer park and an immense garden—enough space perhaps to think, read and write the words that would directly

The interior second-floor hallway of Gunston Hall.

contribute to the ideas and ideals of a new country. Mason did this work, like all the other founding fathers in Virginia, by running his plantation with the labor of enslaved people.

Architecturally, Gunston Hall tends to underwhelm visitors with its façade. The house is made of brick, erected by his enslaved community of laborers or enslaved people who were rented out for the task, a common practice. It is rather horizontal and plain, but it is surprisingly spacious and airy once inside. A trick of the architecture is perhaps something George Mason enjoyed. A superb tour guide pointed out, for example, that when you stand in a certain place in the front hallway, you can view three successive layers of rounded arches on the first, second and third floors. Manipulating the eye is something common enough, but it happens without you noticing it. A brand-new, one-acre riverside garden is currently under construction, with a huge, whitewashed fence surrounding the new plantings, just as it did during the Mason era. Archaeological excavation is a continuous process at Gunston Hall. A family cemetery is a walk down a tree-lined path on the site, containing the grave of Mason and his wife and other family members. More trails lead away from the home and toward the water. A bike rack outside the visitor center is helpful for those biking between the natural and historical places in Mason Neck. Picnic tables are available, but food is not, so pack what you need.

Elizabeth Hartwell Mason Neck National Wildlife Refuge
High Point and Gunston Road
Lorton, VA 22079
www.fws.gov/refuge/mason_neck

When entering the Elizabeth Hartwell Mason Neck National Wildlife Refuge, you might think to yourself: why is a wildlife refuge part of a book about local history? There are many layers of public history to discover here, intertwined with the natural history of the area. Named for local resident and crusader Elizabeth Hartwell, the unique peninsula might have become a planned community and airport if not for her efforts. In the 1960s, when women were not in leadership positions in environmental organizations, federal or otherwise, Hartwell, through her activism, convinced the government of the preciousness of the site where bald eagles are often seen. Today, the Elizabeth Hartwell Mason Neck National Wildlife Refuge is administered by the U.S. Fish and Wildlife

Service, which means that amenities are limited in the green space. There are four miles of walking trails that allow access to visitors, but biking is not allowed. In an attempt to keep the natural area as pristine as possible, fishing, hunting, camping and fires are not allowed.

Walking farther into the wildlife refuge, past old forests where owls are sometimes seen, is a journey that encapsulates some of what Virginia may have been like before widespread European settlement occurred. The trails lead to water-viewing balconies, where water birds and aquatic life can be seen. The High-Point Multi-Use Trail is a paved walking and biking trail that connects Gunston Hall to Mason Neck State Park while traversing the Elizabeth Hartwell Mason Neck National Wildlife Refuge. Thus, this three-tiered green space in Mason Neck is a great place to see the relationship between history and nature over many hundreds of years.

Mason Neck State Park
7301 High Point Road
Lorton, VA 22079
masonneck@dcr.virginia.gov

The Virginia State Park System is considered one of the best in the United States. More than forty state parks are located throughout the commonwealth, from the Atlantic Ocean to the Blue Ridge Mountains, and the organization calls its properties held in the public trust a "tonic for the mind, body, and spirit." Many state parks, including Mason Neck, have preserved historic viewsheds, landscapes and historic sites and have prevented development from encroaching too close to precious environments that support wildlife as well as human recreation. Mason Neck State Park is one of those places, combining history and nature so that the majority of land on the "neck" or peninsula of land jutting out into Occoquan and Belmont Bays and named for the George Mason family is open to the public, providing extended green spaces that connect to the Elizabeth Hartwell Wildlife Refuge and George Mason's Gunston Hall. Mason Neck State Park is located on the Star-Spangled Banner National Historic Trail. For more information on this land-river trail, see www.nps. gov/stsp/index.

Lucy Burns Museum
Workhouse Art Center
9518 Workhouse Way
Lorton, Virginia 22079
www.workhousearts.org/lucyburnsmuseum

Just twenty miles south of Washington, D.C., there is a historic site so complex and layered that you need to spend a full day here. Lorton, a lightly populated area of South Fairfax County, was selected for its proximity to the capital city and its open agricultural land for a new prison in 1910. The Washington, D.C. Department of Corrections used the site for more than ninety years, and it was here, in 1917, that seventy-two women, including National Women's Party leader Lucy Burns, were arrested after picketing in front of the White House for women's suffrage. In American history, they were the first to ever do so. Although the Workhouse was intended by President Theodore Roosevelt to be a model of progressive-era penal reform, where the "moral, mental and physical fiber of prisoners were remade" through a program emphasizing healthy living through hands-on activities in the outdoors, such as growing vegetable gardens and tending animals,

Suffragist Lucy Burns being force-fed at the Occoquan Workhouse in Lorton, Virginia.

173

the experience for the suffragists was violent. Burns was force-fed, which involved being held down in a chair while a rubber hose was pushed down her throat to force her to ingest a milk concoction. A re-creation of this event can be seen if you take the "behind the scenes" tour of the museum, which costs five dollars and allows visitors to walk through an intact cellblock. The mannequins are outdated, but the effect is still chilling—a spot of blood splatters Burns's face and clothing. This kind of inhumane treatment, again, was all because women wanted the right to vote.

The Lucy Burns Museum gets a lot of attention these days because of the recent centennial celebration of the Nineteenth Amendment, which did grant women the right to vote—President Woodrow Wilson's mind changed after news broke of the treatment of the suffragists at the prison—but it is not the only story from the workhouse by a long shot. There are ninety-one years of prison history to discover here; half of the Lucy Burns Museum is devoted to that larger story of incarceration, while the other half of the museum focuses on the suffragists.

After the prison's closure in the first decade of the new millennium, the D.C. Workhouse Prison was reborn as the Workhouse Arts Center. Its large, grassy courtyard—you can't get away from Jeffersonian architecture in Virginia—is surrounded by brick buildings and archways, containing entry points to a series of artist galleries and studios. In the farthest corner of the complex (Building No. 2) is the entry to the Lucy Burns Museum, but there are open studios and galleries all along the green yard. Farther out from the brick campus proper are the remains of the multiple buildings that comprised the entire prison complex, including watch towers that stand sentinel and silent. Murals and works of art dot the landscape, and a walking/biking trail can be found at the back of the complex, connecting visitors to another site with prison and suffragist history.

Occoquan Regional Park
9751 Ox Road
Lorton, VA 22079
www.novaparks.com/parks/occoquan-regional-park

Occoquan Regional Park, managed by the Northern Virginia Park Authority (NOVA Parks) is billed as a "historic riverside reserve with trails." A five-kilometer loop trail snakes through the park, opening up to different vistas and natural areas. It is that and much more, and there is a lot of history to see here. Surveying the scene, a charming open space located on the Occoquan River spreads open in front of you. Kayaks and boats actively use the free boat ramp, and the winding walking trails are full of adults, kids and dogs. Recreational areas and multiple shelter sites for outdoor grilling give the sense of a pleasant spot to spend time "lazing on a summer afternoon," as the song goes. But this area began life as the first spot where prisoners landed after being shipped down from the crowded, dilapidated prison in Washington, D.C. Prisoners landed here and began clearing the land, preparing roads, eventually building the first timber-frame workhouses. Soon enough, they would build gigantic beehive kilns for brickmaking. A brand-new building on the site, which includes the "1608 Room" with artifact display cases, supports visitors learning about the natural and cultural environment and people Captain John Smith found during his explorations of the Occoquan and Potomac Rivers.

BEEHIVE KILN

The beehive kiln built by the workhouse prisoners is really a sight to behold. It sits on a thoroughly redeveloped landscape, next to a brand-new riverside recreational building meant for events and weddings. The working brick kiln would have, instead, been a messy, smoky site, with men in the blazing hot sun preparing the red Virginia clay. There were many kilns lining the property at one time, but only this one survives. Fortunately, an opening

An intact beehive kiln that once served the Occoquan Workhouse in Lorton, Virginia. Today, it is located on the grounds of Occoquan Regional Park.

in the kiln allows visitors to see how clay bricks were stacked, row upon row, horizontally and vertically, filling the domed space. These bricks were used to rebuild the workhouse prison complex in the 1920s and 1930s, when the selected architectural style was Colonial Revival. A few hours away, in Colonial Williamsburg, the Colonial Revival model project for all of Virginia and well beyond, is coming back to life with plenty of brickwork for sidewalks and structures. In Lorton, the new bricks were used to build the needed structures across the 3,200 acres of the prison complex land and special projects, such as the barrel-vaulted arch (see the following section). Now you know why the close by café on the river is called Brickmakers Café.

BARREL-VAULTED ARCH

One of the standing structures made by prisoners with beehive kiln bricks is this beautiful and unusual barrel-vaulted arch, apparently the only one in the commonwealth. If you've ever been to Natural Bridge near the Blue Ridge Mountains, you have a sense of how this man-made bridge/tunnel looks. A wide opening allows for passage below and is complemented across

A barrel-vaulted arch made by people jailed at the Occoquan Workhouse. It was constructed from bricks made in the nearby beehive kilns.

the top of the structure with another passageway (in other words, traffic can move in two directions at the same time). At Natural Bridge, walkers traverse under the bridge while cars drive over it. Either way, the barrel-vaulted arch is a design that dates to classical antiquity and was beloved by the Romans, who built triumphal arches and used barrel-vaulted arches in iconic buildings, such as the Colosseum. The patina of years exposed to the elements and the glow of the sun give the bricks a worn but warm sense. Used today for recreational purposes—the Fairfax Cross County Trail, as well as the Greenway Trail, run under the arch—the structure is something to see, an evocative reminder of both the distant and not-so-distant past.

Turning Point Suffragist Memorial
Occoquan Regional Park
Lorton, VA
www.suffragistmemorial.org

This book ends with the one of the newest works of public art and public history to be installed in Alexandria and South Fairfax County. The Turning Point Suffragist Memorial was dedicated on May 16, 2021, after a long year of waiting due to COVID-19. The new memorial is one of a number of new monuments dedicated to the women's suffrage movement across the United States. New York City, for example, installed the Women's Rights Pioneers Monument in Central Park in 2020, while Richmond, the capital city of the commonwealth, installed the Virginia Women's Monument in 2019, honoring women's history, including Virginian suffragists. The Turning Point Suffragist Memorial was intended to be part of the national commemoration of the Nineteenth Amendment in August 2020, but the pandemic, of course, extended its completion. And still, in fact, there are a few things to do at the new memorial site, a series of engraved capstones to the pillars rest on the ground close by.

The words *turning point* in the title of this memorial highlight the role of the Night of Terror in August 1917, when suffragist Lucy Burns and other suffragists, arrested at the White House, were jailed in Washington, D.C., and here in Lorton at the federal prison known as the workhouse. The suffragists were treated harshly. Some, such as Lucy Burns, were force-fed, and some were beaten. News of the treatment toward the women was intentionally leaked to the media. Outrage from the public was swift and felt deep within the White House itself; President Woodrow Wilson,

The Turning Point Suffragist Memorial in Occoquan Regional Park.

antiprogressive in his views toward women and beholden to the men who had elected him, eventually turned in his feelings toward the Nineteenth Amendment and signed the legislation enabling the passage of the constitutional amendment.

The Turning Point Suffragist Memorial takes some time to take in due to the many parts and pieces presented. First, the idea is to walk through the black iron gates and white pillars, re-creating the sense of the sacredness of what is inside (in 1917, it was the White House). Inside is the story of women and their pursuit for equality. Bronze statues of Black and white suffragists greet you, and a large wall lists suffragists from across the country, state by state. Finally, centered at the far end of the walkway is an open-air rotunda with another statue inside, this one of Carrie Chapman Catt (1859–1947), who raises her arm to greet her audience. Around the rotunda are a series of nineteen interpretive panels, describing the long road to suffrage equality and highlighting the problems with the women's suffrage movement in terms of the lack of recognition white women gave to Black women who were also fighting for their rights.

The special thing about the Turning Point Suffragist Memorial is that visitors are able to see an authentic section of the historic White House fence, the same fence that appears in many of the black-and-white images of women picketing the White House in 1917. For whatever reason, the memorial designers placed this fence section behind the other parts of the installation, but there is a circular concrete path to follow, so don't forget to see the "real" historical object.

BIBLIOGRAPHY

I n addition to the books discussed in the text and more listed below, there are other sources in which to find historical information and images about Alexandria.

PLACES FOR RESEARCH

Local History/Special Collections for the City of Alexandria
Alexandria Library
717 Queen Street
Alexandria, VA 22314
www.alexlibraryva.org/lhsc

National Register of Historic Places, National Archives Catalog
www.archives.gov/research/catalog

Office of Historic Alexandria
220 North Washington Street
Alexandria, VA 22314
www.alexandriava.gov/Historic

Virginia Department of Historic Resources, Historical Highway Marker Program
www.dhr.virginia.gov/highway-markers/

Virginia Room
Fairfax County Public Library
10360 North Street
Fairfax, VA 22030-2514
https://www.fairfaxcounty.gov/library/branches/virginia-room

BOOKS

Arnold, Scott David. *A Guidebook to Virginia's Historical Markers*. Charlottesville: University of Virginia Press, 2007.

Bah, Char McCargo. *Alexandria's Freedmen's Cemetery*. Charleston, SC: The History Press, 2019.

Bah, Char McCargo, Christa Watters, Audrey P. Davis, Gwendolyn Brown-Henderson and James E. Henson Sr. *African Americans of Alexandria, Virginia*. Charleston, SC: The History Press, 2013.

Bulova, Gretchen. *Gadsby's Tavern*. Charleston, SC: Arcadia Publishing, 2015.

Combs, George K., Leslie Anderson and Julia M. Downie. *Alexandria*. Charleston, SC: Arcadia Publishing, 2012.

Cressey, Pamela J. *Walk and Bike the Alexandria Heritage Trail, A Guide to Exploring a Virginia Town's Hidden Past*. Sterling, VA: Capital Books Inc., 2002.

George Washington's Mount Vernon Official Guidebook. Washington, D.C.: Mount Vernon Ladies' Association, 2019.

Maas, John R. *George Washington's Virginia*. Charleston, SC: The History Press, 2017.

Madison, Robert L. *Walking with Washington, Walking Tours of Alexandria, Virginia*. Baltimore, MD: Gateway Press, 2005.

Pope, Michael Lee. *Hidden History of Alexandria, D.C.* Charleston, SC: The History Press, 2011.

Seale, William. *A Guide to Historic Alexandria*. Alexandria, VA: City of Alexandria, 2000.

Weincek, Henry. *The Smithsonian Guide to Historic America, Virginia and the Capitol Region*. Washington, D.C.: Smithsonian Books, 1989.

INDEX

World War I 74, 88, 124, 149,
        154, 164
World War II 51, 68, 74, 75, 80,
        126, 152, 165
Wright, Frank Lloyd 142, 145,
        146, 152

Z

Zouave 116

ABOUT THE AUTHOR

aura A. Macaluso researches and writes about monuments, museums and material culture. She has a PhD from the Humanities/ Cultural and Historic Preservation Department at Salve Regina University. She is currently writing her first book of creative nonfiction; her work can be found at www.lauramacaluso.com. She lives in a circa 1880 house in the historic village of Boiling Springs, Pennsylvania, known for its abolitionist founder, Daniel Kaufman; its spectacular trout-filled river called Yellow Breeches; and the Appalachian Trail, which passes through the center of town and by the bubbling lake.

Visit us at
www.historypress.com